ANDREW JOHNSON—
PRESIDENTIAL SCAPEGOAT

Andrew Johnson —

PRESIDENTIAL SCAPEGOAT

A BIOGRAPHICAL RE-EVALUATION

by Margaret Shaw Royall

An Exposition-Banner Book

EXPOSITION PRESS   NEW YORK

EXPOSITION PRESS INC., 386 Fourth Avenue, New York 16, N.Y.

FIRST EDITION

Dedicated to my grandfather, Alexander Shaw,
and to my grandmother, Felicia Margaret Shaw,
whose plantations were located in Mecklenburg
County, Virginia, and Warren County, North Carolina,
on both banks of the wide and muddy Roanoke.
The Reconstruction Era of Grant's Administration
destroyed both my grandfather's life
and his fortune.

ACKNOWLEDGMENTS

Grateful acknowledgment is due to Mr. Lemuel Carter, a Confederate veteran; Mrs. Philip Love, widow of a Confederate veteran; Mrs. John Hill Shaw, daughter of George Walton Hardy and mother of the author; Mrs. Robinson of Goldsboro, North Carolina, widow of the editor of the *Goldsboro News-Argus;* and "Aunt" Martha Shaw, a former slave; "Uncle" Russell Shaw, a former slave; for valuable information obtained in conversations with them.

I am also indebted to Mr. Lucile Farnsworth, a former resident of Greeneville, Tennessee, who in his later life lived near Plant City, Florida, for the words of the ditty that Andrew Johnson sang in a rich baritone in regard to "coming to Andrew Johnson's tailor shop, to get a broad tail blue."

To Colonel E. C. Reeves, I am indebted for the quotation, "Although Mr. Johnson was not a licensed attorney . . ." and some other facts contained in Chapter XXX of this book.

PREFACE

THIS IS INTENDED as a simple biographical narrative of the lives and struggles of Andrew and Eliza Johnson. Although historical facts have been strictly adhered to, an effort has been made to include every pertinent, poignant personal fact about these two people who have often been misunderstood and, too often, unjustly criticised.

Volumes have been written about Nancy Hanks and her son, Abraham Lincoln. However, probably in as true a sense, there would have been no such man as the seventeenth president of the United States in the person of Andrew Johnson, if he had not met and married Eliza McArdle, then a girl of seventeen, who taught him to write and figure. He could read at the time that he married her.

When I was a girl in college, too many years ago for me to care to calculate, I was impressed with the fact that historians had been unjust to the man who had inherited not only Lincoln's duties but his enemies, also.

James Ford Rhodes describes Johnson's birth and origin thusly: "Born in the midst of degrading influences, brought up in the misery of the poor white class, he had no chance for breeding, none for book education, none for that half-conscious betterment which comes from association with cultivated and morally excellent people. It is said that he never went to school for a day." This is from Rhodes' *History*, volume V, page 517. Somehow my palate for snobbery cannot quite digest this. For this reason and for a long felt appreciation for one of the most unjustly treated characters in our history, this small book has been written. I have often wondered in what way the martyred Lincoln could have had a chance for breeding which Johnson did not have. Yet Rhodes thought that, "Of all men in public life it is difficult to conceive one so ill-fitted for this delicate work." Thus he referred to Johnson when he acceded to the presidency on April 15, 1865.

If Thad Stevens and Charles Sumner, as well as Henry Ward Beecher were morally superior to Andrew Johnson, then history should be rewritten now. Sumner's wife left him after a sojourn of less than a year. Thad Stevens lived openly with a mysterious "Miss Smith," his colored housekeeper, whom he did not marry but who had him buried in a Negro cemetery in Lancaster, Pennsylvania and Henry Ward Beecher admitted at a judicial hearing that he was guilty of calling at the home of his friend, Theodore Tilton, editor of *The Independent* many times in Tilton's absence, and there he had kissed Mrs. Tilton "very much."

One cannot help but wonder if the accusers who were so sure that Andrew Johnson liked a drink too well, did not themselves like the selfsame brandy a mite more than he. Surely Grant had a healthy appetite for liquor. Such were Johnson's detractors.

If this be historical gossip, then let's make the most of it.

M. S. R.

CONTENTS

ANDREW JOHNSON —
PRESIDENTIAL SCAPEGOAT

I : THE CAROLINA YEARS

IN 1808 RALEIGH was more than a trading post. It was the capital city of the great state of North Carolina and nearly a thousand people lived within its boundaries. Besides its courthouse where John Marshall held circuit court, there were taverns, tailor shops, churches and livery stables, as well as the Raleigh *Star*, owned by Colonel Thomas Henderson. Peter Casso's Tavern stood on the main North and South Road, just to the southeast of the Capitol. Its bar was one of the best and its stable could accommodate forty horses at a time. Peter Casso employed a handy man, one Jacob Johnson, an Englishman who lived with his family in a modest house in the lower corner of the tavern property.

Johnson had been born in Northumberland, England and had emigrated from Newcastle to Boston about 1794 or 1795, leaving behind a brother, Thomas, a sister, Isabella and several other sisters. He had been a house carpenter but had decided to try his fortunes in America. Misfortune overtook the ship in which he sailed, when it was overtaken by a French privateer but he and two other passengers managed to make their way to the American states. He finally reached Raleigh about the year 1800.

There the young Englishman met a Scotch-Irish girl, Mary McDonough, called "Polly" and they were married some two years later. He was more than a porter, but he was neither a clerk nor a bartender. At different times he served as constable, sexton of Christ's Church and Captain of the State Militia. To this union were born two sons, one in about the year 1803, a blonde, freckled-face stout boy, whom the parents had named William and a second child born on a stormy night, December 29, 1808, who was dark of complexion with black eyes and hair and who was named Andrew.

Sometime in 1811, Jacob Johnson who was well liked by his fellow townsmen, although he well realized that he was considered a "mudsill," joined a fishing party on Walnut Creek. Colonel Henderson, editor of the Raleigh *Star*, two other companions, Pearce and Callum, and Johnson made up the party. All had too much to drink from Peter Casso's tavern and in such a mood Colonel Henderson began to rock the boat, causing it to upset. Henderson and Callum went to the bottom and Jacob Johnson dived for them and succeeded in rescuing them. William Pearce, the other member of the party, was rescued from shore. As a result of the rescue efforts Johnson's health became so impaired that a year later in January 1812, he died. He collapsed while tolling the statehouse bell for a funeral and he was buried in the Citizen's Cemetery.

Previously Polly Johnson had worked as a seamstress and laundress especially caring for the linen of the North Carolina Supreme Court members, among whom was John Marshall. This scant income was scarcely enough for the subsistence of herself and two small sons. William was now nine and Andrew a little more than three. It is no wonder that she married again, probably thinking that she could not further depress her status. Her choice of a second mate was Turner Dougherty, a worthless ne'er-do-well, although a good natured man of happy disposition. She had scant time to spend on supervision of young Andy but, unperturbed, he spent hours at games with boys in the neighborhood, playing "Cat and Bass Ball and Bandy." However this did not satisfy him and he fell into the habit of visiting the tailor shop of James J. Selby. He liked to listen to the reading aloud to the apprentices and journeymen, who sat cross-legged, sewing and cutting, while a paid reader read newspapers, novels, poems and Congressional debates for hours on end. It was not unlike the "blab school" of that era. The boy was especially noticed by Tom Lomsden, one of the journeymen, whom Andy pestered out of work hours to read to him, for at this time Andy did not know one letter from another. He was approaching ten years of age, when Selby, realizing that business was brisk, decided that he might need another apprentice and so took the boy legally as a bound apprentice. A legal document was drawn up, signed by Andrew's stepfather, Turner

Dougherty, and signed by his mother with a cross mark. However it is a matter of knowledge that her first husband, Jacob Johnson, was able to write and wrote to his family in England after coming to the States.

Under the apprenticeship law Selby was entitled to Andrew's services until he became of age with no salary and in lieu of salary he was to teach him the trade of tailoring, clothe, and feed him. If he should run away, he could be brought back. His master was entrusted also with disciplinary duties even to the extent of flogging, not unlike the status of a slave. Andy was a wild harum-scarum boy, of restless disposition, who tore his clothes, especially in climbing picket fences. However within the next several years he learned the tailoring trade and doubtless how to read.

From time to time he got into scrapes. One Saturday night in June 1824 Andy and another apprentice threw rocks at the windows of a certain Mrs. Wells, mother of two sprightly daughters. On the following day, Mrs. Wells learned the names of the boys who had done the damage and sent word that she intended to prosecute them. The boys became frightened and ran away that night, accompanied by Andy's brother, William, who was also apprenticed to Selby. Many years later W. W. Jordan, friend and neighbor of Andrew Johnson in Greeneville, was told by Johnson that Selby was a hard and cruel master.

The master tailor promptly advertised for the return of the Johnson boys thusly:

> Ran away from the Subscriber on the night of the 15th instant, two apprentices, legally bound, named William and Andrew Johnson. They went off with two other apprentices, advertised by Messrs. Wm. and Chas. Fowler. When they ran away they were well clad in blue cloth coats and new hats, the maker's name in the crown of the hats, is Theodore Clark. I will pay the above reward ($10.00) to any person who will deliver said apprentices in Raleigh or I will give the above Reward for Andrew Johnson alone.
>
> All persons are cautioned against harboring or employing said apprentices, on pain of being prosecuted.

This was dated June 24, 1824 and appeared in the Raleigh, N. C. *Star* on June 26, 1824. The original is now in the North Carolina State Historical Association files in Raleigh.

However, they were not apprehended and they made their first stop at Carthage in North Carolina some seventy-five miles south of Raleigh. Here they set up a tailor shop and managed to establish a trade. Apparently they did not feel too safe within the confines of North Carolina and so moved across the line into South Carolina to the town of Laurens. Here again they established a tailor shop and made a satisfactory livelihood. This was in the fall of 1824 and they stayed there about a year.

Andrew had fallen in love with a young girl in Laurens, Sarah Word, and asked for her hand in marriage. It is said that she returned his love and that she was also beautiful. He is said to have given her a gift of a tailor's goose, which is a tailor's smoothing iron, so-called from the resemblance of the handle to the neck of a goose and also helped her with the design of flowers and fruits on a quilt. He wished to embroider his initials along with hers on the quilt but she forbade this, as being too bold and so only her initials S. W. appeared. According to Sarah Word's granddaughter, the old quilt was still in existence as late as 1930. The idyllic romance of Sarah and Andrew was broken up by her mother, due to his lack of social status. Andrew, mortified and indignant, closed up his tailor shop and returned to Raleigh. Before another year's end Sarah had married William Hance.

It seems also that Selby had written that if Andy would come back and return to work that all would be well. However, when the young apprentice returned, no amicable agreement could be worked out between them. Andy talked to Tom Lomsden, one of the journeymen tailors at Selby's shop, and told him that he was going to try his fortune in Tennessee. Lomsden, who was his friend, described him as "a gawky sort of boy whose clothes never fit him. He wore a little cap and carried a bundle of shirts and socks thrown over his shoulder." It was a bright moonlight night when Lomsden walked out of Raleigh for about two miles with the fatherless boy who wanted to make his fortune in the then West. He told the older man the great things that he hoped to do, but when they shook hands and Andy bade him goodbye, tears ran down his cheeks. In order to cheer him up and perhaps half believing in the possibility of such a miracle, Lomsden told him, "Cheer up, Andy. You'll succeed out there and some day I hope to see you President." The boy's spirits rose and he went whistling down the road.

Fortunately for Andy, a North Carolina man named Brown was moving across the mountains to Tennessee in a train of covered wagons, together with his slaves and household goods. Sometime after he crossed the mountains Mr. Brown saw the boy, sitting by the side of the road with the small bundle of clothes beside him. Andrew asked to be permitted to ride along with them and Brown allowed him to do so. In this way he reached Knoxville, from which point he floated down the river on a flat boat to Decatur, Alabama and walked seventy miles overland to Columbia, Tennessee. This was flourishing farming country and, by chance, also the home of James K. Polk, a fellow North Carolinian who was likewise destined to become President of the United States.

Andrew found employment with James Shelton, the leading tailor of Columbia. Shelton liked young Andrew, who lived in his employer's home for about six months. Some years later Mrs. Shelton took great pride in recounting that she taught him to read but it seems quite positive that he had known how to read since the days of his early apprenticeship in Selby's shop in Raleigh. Undoubtedly, she had helped him with his studies. On the occasion of a visit to Columbia after his presidency, Mr. Johnson was asked if her boast were true. He answered kindly that it was not, but that she seemed to get so much pleasure out of the statement that he had not denied it. "I was glad to give her all the pleasure that I could, for she was a mother to me when I lived with them and worked for her husband," he said.

He probably would have stayed on with the Sheltons but for certain bad news that he received from Raleigh. It may have been that his friend, Tom Lomsden, wrote him, for definitely Polly Dougherty could not write, nor for that matter, could her son, Andrew Johnson. The news was that she was living in direst poverty, her second marriage had not improved her lot in life. Andrew set out by foot for Raleigh again in the summer of 1826. Unfortunately he did not find it possible to find employment for he was legally bound by the articles of indenture of the Raleigh Court to James Selby, who had no idea of releasing him from this obligation. Even Andrew's friend, Litchford, who was somewhat of a politician, dared not employ the boy. Selby would not take Andrew back without certain sureties, which the boy could not furnish. Selby had moved some twenty miles away from Raleigh and Andy walked the twenty miles to the new home of his apprentice-master in an attempt to arrive at either employment or release from indenture, but he was unsuccessful with the surly and stubborn master. Litchford, who had been Selby's foreman in the Raleigh tailor shop, offered to furnish the necessary sureties but Andy was unwilling to let his friend do this. No tailor in the State dared to employ him, and it would be four more years before he could escape from this employment ban.

II : A TRAMP GOES TO GREENEVILLE

ANDREW WAS SEVENTEEN NOW. His brother, William, had gone across the mountains and settled on a farm near the Sequatchie River in southeastern Tennessee. Andrew was the head of the family and this fact seemed not to have been questioned by his easy going stepfather, Turner Dougherty. All were willing to do what Andrew thought best. Therefore in August 1826, the family sold or disposed of whatever possessions they could not pile into a crude cart and set out on the long dusty journey to Tennessee. North Carolina is hot in summer and one hundred degree temperatures are not unusual. Another journeyman tailor, A. D. February from Raleigh, accompanied them for part of the journey and later settled in Jonesboro, Tennessee. Many years later, February wrote to Andrew Johnson, recalling such incidents as "the night the panther knocked the skillet off the fire and you snapped your shot gun at a bear." Polly, wrinkled and swarthy at forty, drove the cart, Turner walked and Andrew led the cow.

They made their way across the Smokies and one Saturday afternoon in September 1826 they arrived in the little village of Greeneville, Tennessee. It was not intended as their final destination but they were weary and needed to rest. They looked about and Andrew saw a pretty young girl standing on the lawn of a rather large house. He walked up to the gate and, as spokesman for the party, asked if she knew where there was an empty house that they might rent for a short time. She knew of a certain cabin, belonging to a Mr. Armitage, and went along with them to point it out and show them the store of the owner.

Andrew rented the cabin from Mr. Armitage and got his family settled. Even at this early date he told his mother that he liked this young lady and intended to marry her. He had not often met with kindness and this was the first help that he had received on this trip. He learned that her name was Eliza McArdle and her father had been a Scotch shoemaker. She and her widowed mother made a livelihood by piecing quilts and making cloth-topped sandals, which trade she had probably learned from her father.

Eliza, too, had been impressed with Andy. When some girl friends chided her with walking up the street with a tramp, calling him her sweetheart, she spiritedly replied that he was quite all right and that she might marry him some day.

Another bit of good fortune attended the renting of the cabin. Storekeeper Armitage had some cloth and since tailors were scarce in small towns he offered to pay Andy to "make up" the cloth. For six weeks Andy did this tailoring for Armitage. At the end of this time they loaded up their cart again and set out, probably, for Columbia, where Andy had friends, but they only went as far as Rutledge, seventy-five miles to the southwest.

Here he was able to rent a small brick law office as his tailor shop. The office had been vacated recently by John Cocke, who had taken his seat in the Federal House in Washington.

Perhaps he could not forget Eliza McArdle, for at the end of six months, hearing the news that Greeneville's only tailor had moved away, the little family moved back to Greeneville. They were "mudsills" according to the social classifications in North Carolina. To explain this classification it is necessary only to say that the homes of the poor and humble, in early days, usually had dirt floors and therefore the door sills were made of mud.

However this did not prevent the romance of Eliza McArdle and Andy Johnson from blossoming and they were married the following spring on May 17, 1827 by Squire Mordecai Lincoln, justice of the peace and a cousin of Abraham Lincoln. The groom was not yet nineteen and his bride seventeen. She had soft hazel eyes, nut brown hair, a fine Grecian nose and tall graceful form. She was described as a beautiful woman with intelligent expression and pleasing address.

In a small building that had two rooms Eliza and Andy set up housekeeping. The tailor shop was conducted in the front room, but it was all their own. There is no doubt that at the time of their marriage the young tailor could scarcely write his name—but he could do that and he could read. He could read as early as his sojourn in Laurens, South Carolina, for he was remembered by a man who lived in the same boardinghouse with him as "always having a book before him." Mr. Litchford, Selby's foreman in the tailor shop, believed that Andy knew his *ABC's* before he was apprenticed to Selby at the age of ten but Mr. Litchford thought he probably taught him to read. Dr. Hill of Raleigh, who often read certain extracts from speeches of orators of the past to the workingmen of his town during their noon hour, once promised Andy a copy of the *United States Speaker* if the boy could prove that he could read it. The boy earned the copy and brought it with him over the mountains from North Carolina to Tennessee.

Now his girl bride undertook to teach him to write and the

rudiments of simple arithmetic. Greeneville had no public library, but he was able to borrow from the few private libraries and benefited from two small colleges then struggling for existence in this mountainous community. One educator, Dr. Hezekiah Balch, had come across the mountains from Mecklenburg County, North Carolina to found Greeneville College in 1794 about the time that Andy's father had come across the Atlantic in the vessel attacked by a French privateer. Greeneville College was the first institution of higher learning south of the Ohio River and west of the Alleghenies. In 1818 Dr. Samuel Doak, a Presbyterian minister of the dour, old school type, moved to Greene County from Washington County, where he had been president of Washington College, and established Tusculum Academy some four miles from Greeneville. He had brought with him what was a large library for that day and time, but it was largely on the subjects of church history and theology. Both of these colleges were in full operation when Andy came across the mountains with his cart and cow in September 1826.

Both colleges had flourishing debating societies and the young tailor soon affiliated himself with the Polemic Society of Greeneville College and was known to walk the four miles back and forth to the campus several times a week. Students there remembered him for his fascinating manner, ability to make friends and for his natural talent for oratory. Some, however, remembered his early efforts as those of a timid speaker, afraid of his own words.

He did make friends nevertheless, two of whom remained his friends throughout life: one, Blackstone McDannel, a plasterer of excellent reputation and the other, Sam Milligan, a graduate of William and Mary College, who was teaching at Greeneville College. Mr. Milligan was not a public speaker himself but he was an excellent coach and he became young Johnson's friend and political mentor. A debating society began to meet in Andy's tailor shop. He would employ a bright school boy to read to him and his assistants daily for fifty cents a day, and the reading was not novels, but debates, Jefferson's messages and over and over again the Constitution of the United States. College students and townsmen alike came, especially on Saturday night when a special subject for debate was selected.

This was in the day before sewing machines, all stitching being done by hand; but Johnson was a good tailor and he employed only competent workmen. From 1827 until 1831 Andy and Eliza Johnson lived in this fashion and in this rear room a son and daughter were born: Charles, his first son, who later became the unfortunate Dr. Charles; and Martha, his first daughter, who in 1865 became the mistress of the White House for her father.

By the practice of rigid economy, after four years he and Eliza began to consider the purchase of a home and on February 24, 1831 he attended a Court sale and purchased a dwelling, paying about $1,000 for it. Squire Lincoln liked Andy and helped him in many ways ever since the boy had come to town and, now, as town magistrate had obtained a judgment on a piece of ground on Water Street near the courthouse. When the lot was put up for sale young Andy bid it in for a small sum. On the lot was a small blacksmith shop, which was included in the sale. Not long afterward he heard of the sale of a Main Street building, which he bought and with the help of some fellow townsmen rolled it bodily up a block and a half to his newly acquired lot. This latter building he changed into the tailor shop for which he was long known. Now the debates were held in this new shop.

Andrew Johnson was a small man only about five feet ten inches in height, of dark complexion and with black eyes and hair. He was hard working and thrifty. His modest business sign simply proclaimed: "A. Johnson, Tailor." But somehow, someway between the years 1827 and 1843 he managed to purchase and pay for "one of the best residences" in Greeneville, his tailor shop, a brick store building and a farm of more than a hundred acres. He established his mother and stepfather on this farm. It may be said with some truth that Turner Dougherty was a worthless sort, but perhaps there has never been a more sincere and ardent admirer of his stepson than he. Whenever there was a public debate in which Andrew took part, Turner was an interested spectator and champion of sorts. Scrubbed and shining, he would appear, ready to fight all comers who might scoff or criticize the tailor-orator.

Andrew was a Democrat and he loved Greene County and its people. He always told these people that he owed them all that he was and they, in turn, would come out of the mountains to hear his voice. He was regarded as the reincarnation of Andrew Jackson, Old Hickory. Greeneville College had closed in 1828 but he continued his activities in debating societies at Tusculum at the Philomathean Literary Society.

Long before he had moved out of the two room combination residence and tailor shop he was elected as an alderman of Greeneville in 1829. He had a genial tolerance for all men and seemed never to lose his temper. On a certain Saturday night immediately preceding the Monday town election a group of his friends met in the counting room where Alexander Hawthorne, the ring leader, was employed. A tally sheet was drawn up with Andrew Johnson as the first name listed. Seven were to be elected and although Johnson received only eighteen votes, the smallest number of any of the successful candidates, at least two other plebeians were also successful. His friend, Blackstone McDannel, a plasterer and Mordecai Lincoln, a tanner, were successful candidates. The original tally sheet is still in the possession of a great-granddaughter of Blackstone McDannel in Greeneville.

The aristocrats of the town were astounded at the election of the tailor, but he filled the office to their ultimate satisfaction, for he was returned to the council in 1830, and 1831 marked the year in which he was elected mayor, which office he held for three successive terms.

He was proud of his humble origin and championed the cause of the workingmen and artisans of the town. In 1832 the county court made him a trustee of Rhea Academy, which Eliza had attended, and it was truly an unprecedented honor for a twenty-three year old tailor who had never attended school for a day.

III : THE TAILOR POLITICIAN

His thoughts began to turn to the State Legislature. Washington and Greene counties had one representative jointly. The tailor shop debating society had discussed the coming canvass which, in those times, was thoroughly informal. There was neither convention nor caucus. On a Saturday night in the spring of 1835, the crowd gathered in Jones' Store to smoke, chew, spit and swap lies. In a short time Andy announced, "I, too, am in the fight." He was then twenty-seven years old. He was opposed by a wealthy citizen, Major Matthew Stephenson.

In one of his early speeches, the aristocratic major spoke of the useful trades, such as farming, carpentry, and tailoring, allowing that each had its useful niche in society but he insisted that law making required men of experience and wisdom. Andy countered with the observation that working with the hands was an older occupation than law making. Was not Tubal Cain a worker in brass and iron; Joseph, the husband of Mary, a carpenter; the Apostle Paul, a tent maker; Socrates, a sculptor; Archimedes, a mechanic; George Washington, a surveyor and a farmer; General Morgan, a tinsmith; and Adam, a tailor by trade for he sewed fig leaves together to make aprons? If there were no privates, where would our officers be? Some critics claim that he was almost brutal in his assaults and that he harangued Stephenson until many pitied the Major, but nevertheless Johnson was elected by a small plurality.

The first term of Andrew Johnson in the Legislature was not outstanding. He opposed a move to have ministers of the gospel open the sessions with prayer on the grounds of separation of Church and State. He opposed the chartering of the Hiwassee Railroad Company on the ground that railroads were monopolies and would frighten the horses of the farmers. He likewise opposed the issue of four million dollars for the construction of macadamized roads for he argued this legislature had no power to impose such a tax on the people without their consent. Sharpers and swindlers would infest the state and squander the money from the departments. Fist shaking went on but the Whigs carried the bond measure, and Johnson was labelled as the enemy of progress. It is no wonder that he was defeated by Brookins Campbell, who was for internal improvements, in the legislative race of 1837.

Campbell seized on Andy's mistakes and made the most of them, but two years later Andy paid him in kind and defeated him. Andrew Jackson was always Johnson's idol politically and he was piloted by Old Hickory's principles. The Whigs hated Jackson and all that he stood for; they were the rich and aristocratic and had a deep and abiding devotion for the things that were past.

In the spring of 1840 Johnson called the Greene County Democrats in a mass meeting in Greeneville in such a successful rally that it served as a model for an annual Jackson-Johnson Democratic Rally in that mountain center. Andrew Johnson spoke for two or three hours and the mountain people who had come from miles around, by foot or horseback, listened as he stood on a few empty boxes set against the courthouse wall. These people came to believe that Andrew Johnson was the reincarnation of Andrew Jackson. He would begin in a low tone and he did not seek for oratorical effect but interspersed his speech with mountain wit and humor.

He was a compelling public speaker and his power to move the minds of men grew steadily. He was particularly adapted to open air speaking and his words and stories were simple and direct. The high sheriff, Richard Woods, was on hand to preserve order and there was less rotten egg and cabbage throwing than in the days of the councilmanic elections in Greeneville. Woods' especial function was to give a sign by a nod for the audience to begin shouting or laughing.

The Greene County Resolutions prepared by Johnson himself were always read by the county clerk, George Foute. Always somewhere in his speech he would make an appeal to the party "to stand together hand in hand, shoulder to shoulder, foot to foot, to make a long pull, a strong pull together." This reference to the wagoners of the day, their habit of helping one another, would bring war whoops of delight that could be heard for miles. Life and figures of speech were simpler in that day. Late in the afternoon many would visit the grog shops of Greeneville before making their respective ways home, swearing that Andrew Johnson was the greatest man in these United States.

The unknown tailor, born a mudsill, had come a long way. He now had four children, Charles, Martha, Robert and Mary. The last of the brood, Andrew, Jr. always called Frank, was quite a bit younger than the rest. Eliza, his wife, was still a young and pretty woman. Thirteen years of married life, many of which were spent in financial hardship, had had small effect on her and now at thirty, she was still healthy and serenely happy.

Johnson was learning the amenities of politics. In 1840 he was selected as one of the Democratic Electors from the State-at-large. It was a worthwhile honor for in selecting him, James K. Polk, from his own State of North Carolina and a future President, was passed over.

In 1841 he was elected to the State Senate and in 1843 he ran for Congress with the campaign centering around the United States Bank. When, in 1843, he ran for a seat in the House of Representatives, he defeated Colonel John A. Aiken, a prominent lawyer who was an excellent orator from a predominantly Whig district.

By this time Johnson had matured and learned caution. He was in his forty-fourth year, had been married sixteen years and had a family of five children. These were the roaring 'forties, the days of hard cider, of rotten egg and cabbage throwing at local political meetings, and of prearranged concerts of whistling and cowbell ringing to greet speakers on the rostrum.

However, in Washington there was a different scheme of things. There is no record of his attendance at receptions, levees or balls in the nation's capital city. He gave his time to reading

books from the Congressional Library and to the mastery of
the details of public affairs. He gave his time to committee
assignments and, together with his friend, George W. Jones
of Tennessee, he made an impression as "a sentinel at the
doors of the Treasury." He recorded his vote against the crea-
tion of useless jobs and "grabs" of all descriptions.

He was scrupulously honest about taking extra pay of any
nature from the Government. On one occasion he was named
as a member of a committee to investigate a contested election,
which assignment carried with it per diem pay. He refused
the amount of $768 and caused it to be entered into the account
book of the Sergeant-at-Arms of the House of Representatives
that he did not doubt the legality of the charge but did doubt
his moral right to receive more than pay for the actual days
engaged in service and therefore declined to receive the balance.

His first speech was dear to the hearts of the Greene County
Democrats. Nearly thirty years had passed since the Battle
of New Orleans but Andrew Jackson lived until 1845. In this
speech Johnson defended the now aged warrior for establishing
martial law in New Orleans. At the time some citizen had gotten
out of bounds and had been arrested. The irate citizen had
appealed to Judge Hall of the District Court, who had then
issued a restraining writ. With a snort, doughty Andrew Jackson had torn up the writ and the Judge himself had been
escorted ten miles out of New Orleans with the advice not to
return to town until the shooting was over. When the shooting
was over and the good judge had returned to his court room, he
levied a one thousand dollar fine on Andrew Jackson for contempt of court. At some later date a bill had been lost in committee after having been introduced into Congress for repay-
ment of this fine. Andrew Johnson now pleaded that this long
overdue money be repaid with interest and the bill passed with
a bountiful majority.

He argued insistently against an increased tariff, saying that
it was an oppressive system of plundering the masses of the
people for the benefit of a certain class. So far as the Texas

question was concerned, Andrew Johnson was firmly for annexation. His political life closely paralleled his ideals in private life, he was for thrift and the growth of a new nation.

On every idea Johnson was opposed by a young Methodist minister, William G. Brownlow. Brownlow was a Whig and editor of the Jonesboro *Whig*. Although no orator he blasted the campaign and character of Johnson mercilessly. Although Johnson was a Methodist, he defiled him as an atheist, called him a villain and on one occasion openly accused Johnson of having hired a rascally brother of Brownlow to assassinate him.

Perhaps one other charge that hurt Johnson inwardly more than this was the charge that Andrew was not the son of Jacob Johnson but a "by-blow of John Haywood," who was a Judge of the North Carolina Superior Court in 1808, adding as a proof that Johnson strongly resembled a nephew of Judge Haywood. Johnson was justly indignant and journeyed to Raleigh to seek certified information on the matter of his birth and returned with many affidavits to refute this slander.

Johnson defended his religion by saying that he believed in the doctrines of the Bible as practiced by Jesus Christ. Brownlow did not succeed in his accusations against his enemy for Johnson was elected for a second term at the time that a fellow North Carolinian, James K. Polk, was beginning his administration as President. However Polk was an aristocrat, and Johnson prided himself on his plebeian birth and the two men were not friendly. They soon quarreled regarding patronage, and Johnson entirely absented himself from the White House thereafter.

Johnson denounced Polk to friends in Tennessee as being willing to hang an old friend in order to make two new ones, adding that the President was not respected as a man. He wrote often to his old friend, Blackstone McDannel, but began to doubt his long-time friend Sam Milligan. He once said in a letter to McDaniel, when he looked back on his past life and remembered the taunts and jeers and intended slights to him and his family that he wished from his heart that he and his were all blotted out of existence. He added that he was not unmindful of the Sunday-praying scoundrels of Greeneville and concluded by saying that he never wanted to own another foot of dirt in the town while he lived. Surely he must have been sorely tried.

At long last he was able to introduce his Homestead Bill on March 27, 1846. This was his life's ambition—to aid the landless ones, the "mudsills," of which class Johnson knew so much at first hand. He had long advocated Homestead legislation and now the problem of disposition of government land in the far-flung West was important to settlement of the vast area. The Southern representation in Congress had always opposed Homestead legislation. Now nine new territories were seeking statehood and with new states in the West settled by free men, the South's control of Congress would be completely out of balance.

Furthermore the Know-Nothing Party feared that the new lands would be taken up by Catholic immigrants; the railroads wanted government land as bonus payment for road building; and high tariff advocates did not want land sales to abolish the need for revenues from tariffs.

Johnson's Homestead Plan was simple. He advocated dividing the governmental lands into quarter-sections to be given to homesteaders without cost to them, if they would settle and cultivate their land for a certain length of time, usually three years. In 1850 such future enemies as Thad Stevens and Jefferson Davis united in defeating it, but in May of 1852 Johnson succeeded in getting his bill passed in the House. His Homestead Bill was hailed with acclaim in the North, but the Raleigh *Register* termed it, "an infamous and nefarious scheme." The Richmond *Whig* called him the greatest of national humbugs.

But it must be remembered that at this time Johnson was no longer a poor man, but an owner of slaves. He had purchased a black boy, ten year old Sam, who became his lifelong admirer and imitator, and another, William, as well as a Negro girl. Eliza McArdle had not done so badly in marrying her "Tramp." Keeping house in one room even with two children had not worn her down and she was still youthful and happy. She had done well to choose her illiterate tailor sweetheart as a life's partner, even though her husband had little aptitude for society or parties for which he had decidedly had no training. Labor in the South was not easy to get from the free labor market and Johnson's purchases of slaves may have been prompted by need.

Now he had battled for free land for free labor and won. This struck a blow at the whole slave system but, nevertheless, he hoped to enter the United States Senate and continue his battle there.

IV : GOVERNOR OF TENNESSEE AND UNITED STATES SENATOR

JOHNSON HAD CALMED DOWN considerably and had delivered no more anti-Polk speeches. Johnson had courage, eloquence and superior ability and now was employing tact. Even as early as 1852 there is some evidence that he was considered as a presidential possibility instead of Franklin Pierce.

But the Whigs hated him with a deadly hatred and determined to end his political career, if humanly possible. They controlled the Tennessee legislature and so put through a bill which would cut off Greene County from the First District and place it in a district which was overwhelmingly Whig. Ill health also plagued the one time tailor, who suffered from a kidney ailment. This gerrymandering of districts did not spell his doom politically. In a speech in the House he stated that the General Assembly had parted his garments and for his vesture was casting lots. Johnson decided to campaign and run for Governor, so the gerrymandering of the First District proved to be a boomerang instead of an aid to the Whigs.

The state convention met in Nashville, with many opponents put up by jealous enemies. Among others proposed were Isham G. Harris, later Rebel Governor of Tennessee, and Edwin

Polk, but Johnson was endorsed by more county delegates than all of his opponents together. At three test votes the night before the caucus, Johnson had a majority on each vote. Nevertheless the next day, certain leaders made up their minds to offer Andrew Ewing, a Nashville man, as the choice of the caucus. Such a turmoil broke out as the result, with several speakers denouncing the unauthorized caucus, that Ewing withdrew in favor of Johnson, and an opposition leader announced capitulation, declaring that Johnson seemed strong enough to run all the Democrats out of the convention and could run Henry, his Whig opponent, out of the State.

During the campaign Johnson told the voters that he had not been gerrymandered out of Congress but Henry-mandered out and the people believed him with doubtless truth. He also ridiculed Henry as the Eagle Orator, as he was familiarly known but said that the eagle had left no mark on him. Henry caustically replied that this was doubtlessly true as the eagle was a noble bird and would not feed on carrion. An unusually large vote was cast and Johnson won by more than three thousand majority.

He was inaugurated on October 17, 1853 with a speech calling attention to the need for education of the people and better treatment of the laboring classes. No one stood in better position to know this need than he. After two months he sent in his first message, in which he proposed a road building tax, gradual liquidation of the Bank of Tennessee to get the state out of the banking business, a reform of the judiciary and heavier taxes for schools. He was one of the first of the Progressives and he made enemies, for he believed that the laboring man was the bulwark of the Nation.

These were the 'fifties and fighting and pistol play were not unknown and were not an unusual way to settle an argument. There came a day when a poster was erected in Nashville, stating that the Governor was to be shot on sight. It was suggested that a bodyguard be sent to protect him on his way to the Capitol. He refused, saying that if he was to be the target that he wanted no other man to be in the way of the bullet, and he walked alone slowly and deliberately from his home to the Capitol as usual.

On another occasion after he had been nominated for a second term as Governor, he had denounced any Know-Nothing as a loathsome reptile, on whose neck every honest man should put his foot. He was warned not to speak at his next appointment, which was a stronghold of the Know-Nothings, if he wished to live. His own party members urged him not to make this speech. However at the appointed hour he advanced to the desk and laid his pistol on it, and announced that he had been informed that part of the business to be transacted was the assassination of the individual who now had the honor to speak. "So," he continued, "if anyone has come here for the purpose indicated, let him shoot." He placed his right hand on his pistol and held open his coat with the other. After a moment's pause, he announced that it seemed that he had been misinformed and he continued with his speech.

Johnson was re-elected as Governor, due to the increased majorities he received in the rural Protestant counties. In his second inaugural address he declared that the people had never deserted him and, God willing, he would never desert them. His theory was that slavery existed as black in the South and white in the North. He was the favorite son of Tennessee for the presidency and when the state convention met in Nashville in January 1856 a resolution was made to that effect. During this time Negro Sam boasted that he was Mr. Johnson's "fust suvvant" and he constantly imitated his master in speech and dress, wearing Johnson's discarded black broadcloths and silk hats with aplomb. Sam was a gentleman in the strictest sense of the word and accompanied Andrew Johnson to the grave. The two men were constantly together and were friends as well as companions. As late as 1901 Sam was living in Greeneville, having been born about 1830 and purchased by Johnson about 1840. The Emancipation Proclamation had little effect on Sam, by his own choice.

After the Cincinnati Convention Johnson loyally accepted the candidacy of the Pennsylvanian Buchanan and he went on a speaking tour for this candidate throughout Tennessee. The Tennessee Democrats carried the state for the presidential nominee for the first time since Andrew Jackson, as well as both houses of the State Legislature.

Johnson did not want a third term as Governor and early in 1856 the Tennessee Legislature sent Andrew Johnson to the United States Senate. It is to be remembered that at that time this decision was left up to the State Legislature and not to popular vote. It is also to be noted that Johnson never missed an opportunity to speak with contempt of the aristocratic class and to humiliate their leaders publicly, whenever possible. He represented a slave state in the Senate but he had no sympathy with the slave states. Therefore they considered him a plebeian upstart and detested him, although he was easily the most popular man in Tennessee. The majority of the citizens of Tennessee were not slave owners and this was particularly true of eastern Tennessee.

One of his last acts as Governor was to recommend the purchase by the State of the Hermitage, home and tomb of Andrew Jackson, and this was done. His theory of government was firmly placed on two premises, (1) preservation of the Union and (2) states' rights.

In the Senate he protested against the fixing of qualifications of voters in Minnesota by the Federal government, when Minnesota applied for statehood, saying that the government had no power to go into a state and set the qualifications of her voters.

Unfortunately that same year he and his senatorial colleague, John Bell, a Whig, became violently angry with each other. Bell had voted against the Kansas-Nebraska Bill and Johnson had stated that a Senator, whose opinions were in entire opposition to those of his constituents, should resign. The Tennessee Legislature favored the Kansas-Nebraska Bill, and it then passed a re   'ing Bell to resign. Bell answered caustically and Johnson defended the Legislature and in a speech inadvertently called Bell a competitor. Bell replied that Johnson was neither big enough nor good enough to be his competitor. It was rumored that the two would meet in a duel; however, they both apologized but were never friendly again. There is a theory that this enmity was the basis for the fact that Bell had little Union fervor and for that reason supported secession a few years later. If the two had united in friendship, doubtless Tennessee would not have seceded and the War Between the States would thus have been shortened. It is well known historically that the bulk and brunt of the fighting was done in Virginia and Tennessee.

This was in 1857. Johnson had served two terms as Governor of Tennessee, had not stood for a third term and had been sent to the United States Senate by the Tennessee Legislature. There was perhaps no more attractive man physically in the Senate than Johnson at forty-eight.

He is described by Ben Truman, his secretary, as "matchlessly perfect in figure." He was five feet ten inches in height, erect, with broad and deep chest and a head that Charles Dickens described in a letter to the latter's son as "splendidly shaped." His eyes were black, sparkling and described by his secretary as "absolutely beautiful." His hands and feet were small. In 1862 Truman said that Mr. Johnson had never been to the theater, but although he liked circuses and minstrels, he seldom attended such frivolities for lack of time. No wonder Eliza McArdle loved him. There is no historical record of anything that his mother, the Scotch-Irish laundress Polly Dougherty, ever said about her son, after he achieved political prominence. She lived to see this, but did not live to see her son, who had been a bound boy in Raleigh, enter the White House as President.

He usually wore a black broadcloth frock coat and waistcoat, black doeskin trousers and high silk hat. Here, indeed, was no backwoods bumpkin, but a Southern gentleman, both in appearance and manner.

He had been opposed by Major Gustavus Henry, a descendant of Patrick Henry, for the office of Governor of Tennessee. Henry was a Whig lawyer and a brilliant speaker. In a speech he chided Johnson for voting against an appropriation for famine stricken Ireland, as Johnson believed that this would be misuse of public funds which had been collected for other than philanthropic purposes, but it would be an excellent means of influencing the Irish vote. Johnson replied that he proposed to his fellow members in the House of Representatives that they give their salaries for a certain time and when they failed to agree to this, he had given fifty dollars to the cause. On another occasion when Henry, called the Eagle Orator, had been particularly flowery in his oratory, Johnson sang the following ditty in a rich baritone, probably to ridicule himself as well as his opponent; saying that he was indebted to some of his friends in Greeneville for the authorship:

> If you want a brand new coat,
> I'll tell you what to do,
> Go down to Andy Johnson's shop
> And get a long tailed blue.
>
> If you want the girls to love you
> To love you good and true
> Go down to Andy's tailor shop
> And get a long tailed blue.

The dignified Major Henry did not know what to do with such a buffoon.

This farce took place during his first campaign for the governorship. He had sold his tailor shop some years before when he was in the State Legislature. When he was sent to the United States Senate, he said, "I have reached the summit of my ambition." He had been elected on the first ballot. He had now lived thirty-one years in Tennessee, twenty-nine of which had been spent in the political arena. He had been alderman and mayor of his home town, state representative and senator, Representative in Congress, Governor of Tennessee for two terms and now United States Senator.

He was known in Tennessee personally, not as a city politician is known, through the columns of a newspaper, but as a small town layman and street corner politician. There were no secrets about him and certainly no pretense. In the South before the War the mass of the people were as ready to heap honors on this Tennessee mountaineer as the North. It is no wonder that he was put on the ticket with Lincoln and elected as Vice-President in 1864.

He differed from Lincoln in at least two respects: (1) he was not a jokester nor an adept teller of humorous stories, (2) he prided himself on the fact that he was a man of the people and never allowed his associates to forget his pride in his humble origin. Jefferson Davis, while in prison at Fortress Monroe in a conversation with Dr. John J. Craven, the kindly prison physician, described Mr. Johnson as "being one of the people by birth, and remaining so by conviction, continually recurring to his origin, though he was by no means the only Senator of the South in like circumstances. His pride was that of having no pride." Johnson and Davis served in the United States Senate at the same time, but it is to be remembered that the above statement was made by the favored son of Mississippi. Mr. Davis added that Mr. Johnson was indifferent to money and careless of praise or censure, when satisfied of the necessity of any line of action.

It is a well-documented fact that on one or more occasions in the early legislative career of Andrew Johnson his name was intentionally omitted from the guest list of his party's political dinner. Such facts he never succeeded in nor attempted to forget.

V : THREE YEARS AS MILITARY GOVERNOR

As LATE AS DECEMBER 13, 1860 Johnson made a last hopeless attempt toward peace by introducing into the Senate a proposal for amending the Constitution in order to prevent the permanent monopoly of the Federal executive and judiciary by any one section. The outgoing President, James Buchanan, had been born in Mercersburg, Pennsylvania and his immediate predecessors, Pierce and Fillmore, had hailed from New Hampshire and New York respectively. According to Johnson's proposal, the President would be chosen alternately from a slave holding and a free state; senators were to be elected by popular vote; all Federal courts were to be composed of judges, one-third of whom should be elected every fourth year for a twelve year term and all vacancies would be filled half from the free and half from the slave states. It is interesting to note that Johnson was the only senator to retain his seat in the Senate after his state withdrew from the Union.

This alone was sufficient to thrust him at once into national prominence. Furthermore he was possessed by nature with the ideal equipment for a popular champion in such a national crisis. He had a fanatical love for the Union and a life-long hatred for the social and economic system upon which aristocratic Southern leaders proposed to build their government. He was unbridled in speech and relentless in purpose. He was utterly without fear.

On one occasion a crowd groaned and hissed him as he passed through Lynchburg, Virginia by train. He was hanged in effigy in Knoxville, Memphis and Nashville, and citizens were allowed to shoot at his caricature. At Liberty he drove off a mob that attacked his car, at the point of his pistol. But his speeches in the Senate arraigning the Rebels aroused the crowds to demonstrations. Spectators stood in their seats, cheering wildly and throwing their hats into the air.

On March 3, 1862 President Lincoln appointed Andrew Johnson, as military governor of Tennessee and brigadier-general of volunteers. At this time the aristocratic Isham G. Harris had been elected as Governor of Tennessee and remained so during the four year period. Of Johnson, Harris had said, "If Johnson were a snake, he would lie in the grass to bite the heels of rich men's children." It is a well known fact that Mr. Johnson was a lover of children and even small animals. It would be difficult to find many to agree with Mr. Harris.

Jefferson Davis had once asked Johnson, "What do you

mean by the laboring classes?" To which Johnson replied, "Those who earn their bread by the sweat of their faces and not by fatiguing their ingenuity."

In regard to slavery, Johnson had hoped for the eventual disappearance of the institution, as entirely in variance with the principles of democracy and equal opportunity for all men. However, he recognized that it was so deeply rooted in the life of the South and that, in justice to rights lawfully acquired as well as for social stability, it should not be molested as long as it remained in subordination to and in harmony with the government.

He had made a speech in the Senate with the emphatic assertion that the War was waged for the Constitution and the Union, and not against any section or institution. Of this particular speech, Alexander H. Stephens later wrote, "This speech was one of the most notable, as it certainly was one of the most effective, ever delivered by any man on any occasion. I know of no instance in history when one speech effected such results, immediate and remote, as this one did."

Johnson had been appointed and held office as military governor during the pleasure of the President, or until the loyal inhabitants of that state should organize a civil government in conformity with the Constitution of the United States. It was only natural that the fury of the Tennessee secessionists should be turned on this "traitor," who had become the instrument of their subjugation. However, Mr. Johnson did not hesitate to leave the comfort and security of Washington at the President's call and thus enter enemy territory to battle with danger and insecurity for the next three years.

His mail was filled with insults and threats and guerrilla bands hoped to intercept his train and take him south to answer for his "crimes" before he even reached Nashville. At least one elaborate plan to kidnap him by an organized force was sanctioned by General Bragg. One anonymous threat ran as follows: "Go it, Andy, this is your day. But while you are going so high, you must not forget that evry dog has his day And the day is not far advanse when you will have your Just day, and that day cannot ever come untill you are tared and feathered and burnt. We are preparind a knise coat of feathers for that orcation, so when we have the chanse We will turn your black skin read, and then your black friends will not know you."

Governor Isham Harris and the state government had disappeared and fled to Memphis. The vaults of the state bank and the treasury had been robbed, including the funds gathered for the instruction of children. It is to be remembered that in this era and for many years afterward, children of the so-called better class did not avail themselves of public instruction but attended private schools.

The oath of allegiance was tendered to the mayor of Nashville and the city council, who promptly refused it. The Governor then declared these offices vacant, and filled them by appointment and the new council imposed the oath on all municipal officers, including the Board of Education and school teachers. Shortly thereafter ex-Mayor Cheatham was arrested for disloyalty and uttering treasonable language against the Government of the United States. Other victims were ex-Governor Neil S. Brown, Judge Guild of the Chancery Court and the president and cashier of the Union Bank of Nashville. The editor of the *Banner* was imprisoned and the plants of the Methodist and Baptist publishing houses were seized and closed for the propagation of disloyalty. Six ministers, who were accused of preaching treason during their sermons, were summoned before Johnson and requested to take the oath. They refused, but were given time for consideration by their own request. Later all refused to take the oath and five of these were imprisoned. The sixth was paroled due to his feeble health. Shortly afterwards these men were sent south beyond the Federal lines.

"These assumed ministers of Christ," Johnson wrote, "have done more to poison and corrupt the female mind of this community than all others, changing their entire character from that of women and ladies to fanatics and fiends. One of these very ministers, in leaving here for Louisville, told those collected to see him off: 'Don't forget your God, Jeff Davis, and the Southern Confederacy.' This is a specimen of the 'blameless course,' who, in the language of Pollock, are wearing 'the livery of heaven to serve the devil in.'" Several of these ministers were admitted to parole in October after having been arrested in June.

Southern Middle Tennessee was the battlefield of the great armies of the West in every year of the War, and Nashville was in a state of siege during the entire summer of 1862 and was threatened by Hood as late as the winter of 1864.

In the spring of 1862 the circuit and county courts opened as usual in the various parts of Middle Tennessee. To avoid unnecessary annoyance and in order to win for them all the popular support possible, Governor Johnson did not require the officers of the courts to take the oath of allegiance. There was continuous friction between the civil and military authorities and well it might have been. Robbery, theft, arson and murder are ordinarily offenses cognizable by military tribunals. Naturally bridges were destroyed by burning or other means by Confederate sympathizers. A military order was issued that directed that any person destroying a bridge by burning or other methods should be hung, preferably at a point near the bridge that was thus destroyed.

In April 1863, General Veatch, commander of the post of Memphis, appointed a civil commission of three citizens, to hear and determine complaints and suits instituted by loyal citizens of the United States for the collection of debts, the enforcement of contracts, the prevention of frauds, and the recovery of property, real and personal. This commission became the object of violent attack, but continued throughout the War. It was claimed that two of the three commissioners were not residents of the state. Mr. J. M. Tomeny, a radical Unionist, claimed that in one typical case, a claim involving thirty-eight dollars had costs amounting to forty dollars and that the net profits of the commissioners from fees collected in the first three months of operation amounted to $4,500. Personal property was levied on and sold in three days, and no appeals were allowed. Despite contrary opinion, Governor Johnson had power to establish courts in Tennessee; this power having been especially conferred on him by his commission from President Lincoln, which included "the power to establish all necessary offices and tribunals and suspend the writ of habeas corpus."

Andrew Johnson possessed the complete confidence of Mr. Lincoln, doubtless prompted by natural sympathy for a personality, in many respects, resembling his own. He once said: "Andy Johnson has never embarrassed me in the slightest degree."

Complete rules covering Negro enlistments in Maryland, Missouri and Tennessee were promulgated as general orders from the War Department. Slaves were to be classified and treated according to the loyalty of their owners. For every slave enlisted with the consent of the owner, the latter received a certificate entitling him to compensation, not to exceed four hundred dollars for the slave's services, upon proving title and filing a valid deed of manumission. Any loyal owner, who claimed upon oath that his slave had been enlisted without his consent could inspect the enlisted men for the purpose of identifying his property, and if necessity required the retention of the slave, the owner was to receive compensation. For Tennessee, Johnson was empowered to modify these orders, subject to the approval of the War Department. No prominent loyal Tennesseeans opposed the enlistment of Negroes.

A convention in Nashville adopted the following resolution: "Whereas the militia of the state constitutes the military power, which must, when necessary, sustain the civil in the suppression of crime and punishment of evil-doers, all able-bodied males, white and colored, between the ages of eighteen and fifty years, except those afterward exempted, are to be enrolled." The magistrates in the rural districts were to act as commissioners for this purpose. Any justice of the peace who failed to perform his duty was to be sent out of the state. It was now realized that thousands who had remained in non-committal security and inaction, must now declare themselves openly for one side or the other. This was not done in Tennessee until 1864 and the fact that many understood it to be a conscription, rather than an enrollment, caused many recruits to be gained for Forrest and Wheeler, for the Confederacy. Hints were common, especially in West Tennessee, that the system was not fairly administered and that officers in charge exempted rich anti-Union men from service and pressed hard on poor loyal laborers. According to official records, Tennessee furnished to the Union army, 31,092 white soldiers and 20,133 colored troops, not credited on the state quota.

VI : ELIZA DRIVEN FROM HER GREENEVILLE HOME

ON APRIL 8, 1862, President Jefferson Davis placed East Tennessee under martial law. Colonel Church, the Confederate provost-marshal at Knoxville, warned all who had fled to the enemy to return within thirty days. Those who did so were offered amnesty but those who had failed to comply would have their families sent to Kentucky or beyond the Confederate lines at their own expense. It stated "that the women and children must be cared for by husbands and fathers, either in East Tennessee or in the Lincoln government."

At this time, Eliza McArdle Johnson was living in Greeneville with her youngest son, Andrew, Jr., a boy about nine years old, and her younger daughter, Mary, now married to Colonel Daniel Stover of the Union army and Mrs. Stover's children. Mrs. Johnson was an invalid, due to the ravages of consumption. Her older son, Dr. Charles Johnson, was a surgeon with the Union army and was later killed in the Battle of Nashville. His death was due to a fall from a horse in the course of the siege. Her second son, Colonel Robert Johnson, commanded a regiment originally of the infantry, but later transferred to the cavalry service, and was engaged in securing proper horses and equipment for the Tennesseean armies. This was an almost impossible task, as the Confederates had taken almost every animal of value for their own military purposes.

Finally some troops were forced to attempt to use mares, but this experiment worked badly and was abandoned.

Mrs. Johnson remained quietly in her Greeneville home, for certainly the embattled city of Nashville was no place for her. When General Kirby Smith of the Confederate army marched into Greeneville, probably because she was the wife of the Military Governor of Tennessee and also because her home was one of the largest and most substantial in the town, she was advised on April 24, 1862 that her home was needed for military purposes and was ordered to pass through the Confederate lines within thirty-six hours.

She did not comply with this order at once, and lived through distressing circumstances for some months. Stories are told that she was not even solaced by her own townsmen, but rather, neighbors were heard to gossip with such statements as, "Perhaps she will not have such high and mighty airs now." There were instances in which mud and stones were thrown at her windows and definitely her house and family were not accorded protection. East Tennessee was firmly in the grip of the Confederacy. Her home was used as an army barracks. She was driven from her house and finally at her own request, she and her family were sent north in September. Naturally her property and that of her husband was confiscated.

In the darkest days of the Confederacy at least one letter from Andrew Johnson to his beloved Eliza has been preserved. In it he wrote: "I feel sometimes like giving up in despair; but this will not do, we must hold out to the end, this rebellion is wrong and must be put down, let cost what it may in the life and treasure. I intend to appropriate the remainder of my life to the redemption of my adopted home, East Tennessee and you and Mary [his daughter, Mary Stover] must not be weary, it is our fate and we should be willing to bear it cheerfully. Impatience and dissatisfaction will not better it or shorten the time of our suffering." His was a tortured mind and exhausted body. His property had been confiscated, his family in danger and distress, hated and insulted by neighbors. He had been maligned by enemies or rivals and seemingly discredited in organizing his state. He had forsaken the easy and safe duties of civil life for a position involving personal toil and danger.

This letter is one of the few in his own handwriting still in existence. His arm had been broken in a train accident during one of his trips from Washington to Greeneville and a badly set bone permanently interfered with his penmanship after this.

VII : THE BATTLE OF NASHVILLE

THE GARRISON AT NASHVILLE was small. Many troops had been withdrawn for an all-out attack on Corinth by General Buell. The capture of Corinth would mean the control of the railroad connecting Memphis with Richmond and Charleston. Nashville, as well as Lebanon and Murfreesboro were stripped of a regiment. Johnson sent vehement dispatches to Secretary of War Stanton and General Buell, to which Buell replied that the regiments would be replaced by new ones. This promise was not kept. Buell insisted that the Governor's wishes were absurd. General Halleck advised Stanton: "We are now at the enemy's throat, and cannot release our great grasp to pare his toe-nails."

Corinth was abandoned by the Confederates on May 29 and some two weeks later Buell began his long delayed advance on the Memphis-Charleston railroad. His plan was thwarted by the quick action of Confederate General Bragg, who seized Chattanooga before Buell could establish himself there. All during the summer of 1862 the Union army was harassed by daring and successful operations directed at lines of communication and railroad depots. General John Morgan swept the entire interior of the state and surrounded Nashville. Murfreesboro and Lebanon had both fallen, and toward the end of July Nashville was completely cut off from railroad and telegraph communication with the North.

The streets were barricaded on the night of July 21 and citizens were in panic. A thousand slaves of secessionist owners were impressed for work and their masters were required to provide them with tools. The garrison was considerably depleted and rations were low. On this date General Forrest penetrated to within six miles of Nashville. General Nelson, in charge of the defense, had no cavalry, and could only remain behind his fortifications. Even Fighting Parson Brownlow stated: "The indications are that the rebels will have Kentucky and Tennessee . . . if I were Governor Johnson, I would resign on the ground of not being backed up by the government. The administration seems to look only to Richmond and neglects every other point."

To this time belongs a story in regard to Johnson and Colonel Moody, the fighting Methodist parson, who had gone to attend the Philadelphia Conference. The Colonel was in Nashville on the day it was reported that Buell had decided to evacuate the city. He told this story to President Lincoln while on the trip from Philadelphia. Moody had gone in search of Johnson and at the end of the evening, found him in his office closeted with two gentlemen, who were walking the floor with him, one on each side. As Moody entered, they retired, leaving him alone with Mr. Johnson.

Johnson came up to him and with intense feeling said, "Moody, we are sold out. Buell is a traitor. He is going to evacuate the city and in forty-eight hours we shall all be in the hands of the Rebels." Then he began pacing the floor again, twisting his hands and chafing like a caged tiger, utterly insensible to his friend's entreaties to become calm.

Suddenly he turned and said, "Moody, can you pray?"

"That is my business, sir, as a minister of the Gospel."

"Well, Moody, I wish you would pray," said Johnson, and instantly they both went down on their knees on opposite sides of the room. As the prayer waxed fervent, Johnson began to respond in true Methodist style. Presently he crawled on his hands and knees to Moody's side and put his arm over him, manifesting the deepest emotion. Closing the prayer with a hearty "Amen," they arose.

Johnson took a deep breath and said with emphasis, "Moody, I feel better." Shortly afterwards he asked, "Will you stand by me?"

"Certainly, I will," was the answer.

"Well, Moody, I can depend on you; you are one in a hundred thousand." He then began pacing the floor again. Suddenly he wheeled, the current of his thought having changed, and said, "Oh, Moody, I don't want you to think I have become a religious man because I asked you to pray. I am sorry to say I am not, and have never pretended to be, religious. No one knows this better than you; but Moody, there is one thing about it . . . I do believe in Almighty God. I believe in the Bible and I say I'll be damned if Nashville shall be surrendered." And Nashville was not surrendered.

During the last days of the siege of Nashville, a secret committee of citizens sent an appeal to their friends in the attacking army to abandon the assault since the defenders had resolved to destroy the city rather than surrender. Finally on August 21, Bragg sprang the surprise that he had been preparing for Buell. Issuing suddenly from Chattanooga, and deceiving Buell with demonstrations in the direction of Nashville, he struck the Louisville-Nashville Railroad, which was Buell's line of communication and supply, captured Munfordsville, the principal station between the two cities and then marched into Kentucky. On August 30, he sent a dispatch to the Governor, explaining the course he had taken and there followed a series of reasons or excuses for not attacking on account of the supposed greater size of the Confederate forces.

Buell's real designs regarding the defense of Nashville were made the subject of a court of inquiry in November of that year. Andrew Johnson deposed for this court of investigation that it was rumored among Unionists and Confederates alike that Nashville would be surrendered. He stated also that many prominent secessionists returned with Bragg's army in the sincere expectation that they would regain their homes. Johnson had obtained an interview with Buell and earnestly urged the political considerations involved, begging that the city be held at all hazards, or, if absolutely necessary, destroyed, but never surrendered. Buell had replied impatiently that he would conduct his campaign in accordance with his own judgment, regardless of criticism. The credit for saving Nashville is fully accorded to Johnson. The commission accepted Johnson's account rather than Buell's excuses. Some historians do not blame Buell; but in addition to Johnson, the Governors of Indiana, Illinois and Ohio urged the removal of Buell.

The administration and war policy of Lincoln were endorsed and he was renominated for the presidency in 1864. Along with him was nominated Governor Johnson who, "by his unflinching courage and patriotism" had "endeared himself to all American patriots, and by his long public services, especially by the administration of affairs" during his term as Military Governor of Tennessee.

In spite of all the bitterness between former friends and neighbors, there still remained a sense of humor between the soldiers themselves. The immortal Stonewall Jackson was inadvertently shot by one of his own men while he was reconnoitering at the time of the Battle of Chancellorsville. He suffered an arm amputation at a field hospital and was taken to Guinea Station near Fredericksburg, Virginia, in hopes of recuperation. There he succumbed to pneumonia. At this time General Joseph Hooker of the Union army was apparently secreting himself and his forces in a section generally known as the Wilderness. After the Battle of Chancellorsville, he refused to come out to fight.

This conversation took place, at that time, between two opposing pickets one frosty morning. "Where's old Joe?" inquired one Johnny Reb. "Gone to Stonewall Jackson's funeral," was the ready reply. "What is the reason you Johnnies never have any decent clothes?" hallooed the Union boy back. "Ah, we-uns don't put on our best to kill hogs in," was the retort.

VIII : THE MURDER OF MR. LINCOLN

APRIL 1, 1865 FELL on a Saturday. On that day the *Daily Dispatch* of Richmond was published for the last time until December 9 of that year. The owner and publisher was James A. Cowardin and his descendants still live in present day Richmond. Several advertisements that appeared in this last edition are interesting:

> *FOR SALE,* a very fine double-cased gold watch, case beautifully chased, superior workmanship, and warranted in perfect order. Price, $2800.
>
> *RAN AWAY FROM THE SUBSCRIBER:* on the 13th of February, a Negro man, named Robert. Said Negro is about 40 years of age, and a mulatto. Had on, when he left, a brown slouch hat and a brown army overcoat, and is believed to have gone to his home, in Goochland, at Mrs. John Allan's. I will give $100 reward if returned to me, beyond Battery No. 8, or put in jail so I can get him. Thomas Bruton.
>
> *ARRIVAL OF PRISONERS*—Four hundred and odd Yankees prisoners, including a few officers, were brought to this city yesterday afternoon and committed to Libby. Others are expected here during the day.

The last was a news item and confirms the general contention that old Libby Prison continued to receive and care for, after a fashion, a number of Yankee prisoners right to the end of the conflict.

The price of the watch above may be a little surprising, but this was Confederate currency. Yardage for a calico dress at this time cost $125 and Virginia plantation owners kept the amount of currency needed for necessary operations in a wooden barrel, in lieu of a bill fold. There was slight danger of theft of any of this by Negroes for they could buy little with it and merchants would not have accepted it from them in large quantities.

On the next day, Sunday, Jefferson Davis went quietly to

St. Paul's Episcopal Church at the corner of Ninth and Grace Streets in Richmond, immediately opposite the State Capitol. The rector, Dr. Minnegerode was reading the Prayer for the President of the Confederate States, when a messenger slipped quietly to his pew and gave him a dispatch from General Lee. Mr. Davis silently left the church and the congregation was dismissed with the notice that there would be no evening service. That afternoon at about 2 P.M. the Confederate Government left Richmond. At 8:15 the next morning General Weitzel, in command of the Wisconsin troops, entered the city and received the surrender of the city at the City Hall. The offices of the *Dispatch* and *Examiner* were in ruins and the streets in the vicinity of the fire were littered with the debris of household furniture. The armory had been burned and the Petersburg and Richmond Railroad Bridge across the James had nothing left save the pillars.

On Tuesday, President Lincoln entered the city, accompanied by Andrew Johnson, but it was not the entry of a conqueror. There was no martial music, no pompous columns of soldiers, only Lincoln, Johnson, Admiral Porter and three other officers and ten common sailors, who walked a mile and a half through the streets of the fallen city. "With malice toward none; with charity for all;" he had come.

Citizens stayed within their own doors. Not until the return of General Lee and his bedraggled troops did they rush out and press into the hands of the ragged and half-starved troops, the remains of their long-hoarded rations. At that time women rushed out and pressed upon the marching soldiers, still in rags, the best coats of husbands and fathers. In the chill April air some youthful infantrymen mounted these garments on their bayonets to simulate a flag of victory.

Some years before, through an association of Mr. Lincoln with the uncle of Confederate General George Pickett, the former had been the means of securing an appointment at West Point for young Pickett. Now it was reported that General Pickett had been killed at the Battle of Five Forks which, though untrue, was generally believed for some weeks. Richmond had been swept by a surging fire and Pickett's wife and baby were somewhere in that then small city. The servants had all run away, for the most part, and the city was full of Northern troops. The story is told that Mrs. Pickett with her baby on her arm went to answer a knock on her door and looked up to see a tall gaunt, sad-faced man, dressed in ill-fitting clothes, who inquired with typical Yankee accent, "Is this George Pickett's place?"

"Yes, sir, but he is not here."

"I know that, ma'am, but I just wanted to see his place. I am Abraham Lincoln."

"The President," Mrs. Pickett managed to gasp.

"No ma'am, No ma'am, Just Abraham Lincoln, George's old friend."

"I am George's wife and this is his baby," she answered. Then the baby pushed away from his mother and reached out for Mr. Lincoln, who took him in his arms. The baby opened his mouth wide and gave him a dewy kiss.

When the President gave the infant back to his mother, he said, "Tell your father, the rascal, that I forgive him for the sake of that kiss and your bright eyes." He turned away going down the steps and talking to himself; out of the sight of a Confederate woman forever, but leaving the memory of his intensely human eyes and strong sad face.

On July 13, 1863, the Draft Law had been enacted by Congress, which exempted from its provisions all who would make a money payment of three hundred dollars. This law was met in New York by four days of rioting, resulting in the hanging to lampposts of nearly one thousand Negroes and the burning of more than fifty buildings. Ten thousand troops were marched into the city and order was restored.

"The age of rail splitters and tailors. Backwoods lawyers. An insult to the common sense of the people." But Abraham Lincoln had been re-elected and with him, Andrew Johnson, and their plurality was less than six thousand short of half a million votes.

At the time of the inauguration Andrew Johnson had worked hard and long hours as Military Governor of Tennessee and was

slowly recovering from an attack of typhoid fever. He had requested that he be permitted to take the oath of office in Nashville but Lincoln had not approved of this plan. Many cities
on his line of progress to Washington had invited him to speak
but he declined on account of his physical weakness.

On the eve of the inauguration Colonel Forney and other
admirers of the Vice-President elect celebrated this culmination
of the Tennesseean's career with a party at which wine and
oratory flowed freely. The next morning Mr. Johnson was cha-
grined at his unsteady condition; however, he was perfectly
sober. He was staying at the Kirkwood House and rode down
Pennsylvania Avenue on the morning of March 4 with Senator
Doolittle and Hannibal Hamlin, the outgoing Vice-President.
When they entered the Vice-President's room, Johnson, said to
Hamlin, "I am now very weak and enervated and require all
the strength and energy I can get. Can you give me some whiskey?" The effect of alcohol on typhoid convalescents is well
known.

"No," the defeated Hamlin replied. "When I became vice-
president, I gave an order prohibiting the sale of liquor in the
Senate restaurant. But if you desire, I will send across the
street for some."

Hamlin did send for some and Johnson drank "a good pota-
tion." They remained seated for some minutes until it was time
for the ceremony to begin. As he rose Johnson said, "I will
take some more of the whiskey, as I need all the strength for
the occasion I can have."

The heating arrangement of the Capitol was working far
too well that day and in his weakened condition the liquor
played havoc with the Vice-President elect. Throughout his
speech he made repeated references to his plebeian origin and
proceeded to tell each group that the people stood above them.
He proclaimed to the Senators, and the judges of the Supreme
Court that they were but the creatures of the American people.
According to legend, he then turned to the Diplomatic Corps
and thus addressed them, "You, too, gentlemen of the Diplomatic Corps, with all your fine feathers and gewgaws."

Several Senators of the Republican Party began to hide their faces and Sumner covered his face with his hands. Some of the press were too ashamed to write the news account. As President Lincoln left the Senate Chamber to go to the steps of the Capitol to deliver his own Inaugural Address, he turned to the Marshal and said, "Do not let Johnson speak outside."

According to accounts Mr. Johnson went to bed in illness and probably in mortification later in the day. He made no attempt to preside over the Senate. He was taken out to Silver Spring by the Blairs for a needed rest and stayed some two weeks and old Francis Blair became entirely captivated by Johnson before his return. The country as a whole was horrified and the Senate voted to exclude liquor from the Senate wing of the Capitol and voted to drop two Senators from all the standing committees because of their habitual inebriety and incapacity for business.

At Grover's Theater on E Street a ditty was composed:

> At Washington the other day,
> There was a brilliant display,
> For some were drunk
> And some were gay
> At the Inauguration.

> O, was it not a glorious sight,
> To see the crowd of black and white
> As well as Andy Johnson tight
> At the Inauguration.

> There is a place well known to all;
> To Senators both great and small,
> A grog shop called
> "A hole in the wall"
> At the Capitol of the nation.

> And there great Andy Johnson got
> And took a brandy-toddy hot,
> Which made him drunk as any sot,
> At the Inauguration.

And now to wipe out the disgrace,
The President has closed the place
Where Andy Johnson fell from grace,
At the Inauguration.

Most of the newspapers were far from kind in their reporting, especially the New York *World* and the Washington *Times*. However a week later the *Independent's* Washington correspondent noted that the newspaper comments were having a salutory effect on Johnson's conduct and on that of others as well. It was stated that Mr. Johnson was in a shattered condition, resulting from a severe illness and severe labor. It closed with the comment that Mr. Johnson resolved never to give offense to the Senate again, but if he was to keep this noble resolve he must part company with some of the Senate officials or they must throw their whiskey demijohns out of their windows of the official apartments.

Time rushed on. On April 3, Lee began his last retreat and four days later he and General Grant sat in McLeans' house at Appomattox to arrange the terms of the surrender.

Lee was a man of much dignity with an impassive face. He came dressed in full uniform and wearing a sword of considerable value. Grant was dressed in a rough traveling suit, the uniform of a private with the straps of a lieutenant general, and said himself that he must have contrasted strangely with a man so handsomely dressed. They fell into conversation about old army times, each saying that he remembered the other well. After the conversation had run on for some time, General Lee reminded the other as to the object of the meeting and said that he had asked for the interview for the purpose of getting the terms that were proposed to be given his army.

The formal terms were then written out. The officers were to be given individual paroles not to take up arms again against the United States until properly exchanged and each regimental commander was to sign a like parole for the men of his command. Arms, artillery and public property were to be stacked and turned over to officers, except the side arms and private horses and baggage. When General Grant was told that in the

Confederate Army, the cavalrymen owned their own horses, he said that he would instruct the officers to let every man of the Confederate Army who claimed a horse or mule to be allowed to take the animal home with him. At this point Ulysses S. Grant reached his highest point. When the news of the surrender reached the lines, the men began firing a salute of a hundred guns in honor of victory. He at once sent word to have this stopped.

In the afternoon several of General Grant's staff, by permission of General Lee, went over into the Confederate lines and had a pleasant time with old friends. To the McLean House there came officers of both armies in large numbers. Many had known each other at West Point or in some social relationship.

Lincoln held his last Cabinet meeting on April 14. Nine days before William Seward, Secretary of State, had been thrown from his carriage and received serious injuries, which at the age of sixty-four years not only confined him to his bed but caused his fractured jaw to be encased in an elastic wire bandage to hold the bones in apposition. Gideon Welles of Connecticut, Secretary of the Navy, was also at this last cabinet meeting. On Welles' initial appointment he had faced the almost impossible assignment of blockading the Confederate coast from Cape Henry, Virginia to the Rio Grande with only one vessel in all the Northern ports fit for a naval engagement. This did not deter this Connecticut Yankee for, by the end of 1863, the War Department commanded six hundred vessels of war and seven hundred other ships. Seventy-five of these were iron clad. Had not an effective blockade cut off the Southern States from legitimate commerce, the Northern armies would not have been able to subjugate them.

Ulysses S. Grant was also present at this meeting, and was greatly admired at this time. His behavior and generosity to Lee had thrilled both North and South. Three years and ten months before he had been a clerk in his father's hardware store in Galena, Illinois. Although a West Point graduate, in 1854 he resigned from the Army and had tried to run his wife's farm near St. Louis but it did not pay. He then tried to sell real estate in St. Louis unsuccessfully and at thirty-eight he had asked for assistance from his father and had become a clerk in a hardware and leather store of the latter at an annual stipend of eight hundred dollars. At this time he was in debt, shiftless and intemperate and those who knew him both in Galena and St. Louis were wont to avoid him on the street to avoid the embarrassment of refusing him a small loan. Still he had shown capacity when others had failed and had shown great generosity toward an enemy who had surrendered, when he might have easily done otherwise. In judging him harshly, we in the South should never forget this.

After the Cabinet meeting, Abraham Lincoln and his wife went for a short drive on the afternoon of April 14. Mr. Lincoln on this drive said to her, "Mary, we have had a hard time since we came to Washington; and with God's blessing we may hope for four years of peace and happiness and then we will go back to Illinois and spend the rest of our lives in peace."

Mary Todd Lincoln had arranged a theater party for that night to see Laura Keene in *Our American Cousin* at Ford's Theater. Lincoln was not eager to go and General Grant and Mrs. Grant were to have been in the party but had excused themselves because of the desire to see their children in New Jersey. The Lincolns were accompanied by Major Rathbone and a young lady, Miss Harris, instead of the Grants.

Shortly after ten o'clock John Wilkes Booth, an actor, but not in this play, having partaken fully of liquor to give him the necessary courage, sneaked into the presidential box, lifted his Derringer pistol, aiming and firing it directly at the President's head. Briefly he faced the audience, crying "*Sic semper tyrannis,*" which is, alas, the motto of Virginia. His aim was true and the bullet entered the brain of Lincoln. Major Rathbone struggled with Booth, who broke away from him. The President was taken across the street to the home of a Mr. Petersen, where he died the next morning at 7:22.

Mr. Lincoln had several times mentioned that he had a pre-

sentiment that when the war ended that his life would also end. He had mentioned this in July 1864 to a correspondent of the Boston *Journal* in these words: "I feel a presentiment that I shall not outlast the rebellion. When it is over my work will be done."

IX : THE PLAN OF THE MURDER
AND ITS AFTERMATH

THERE HAD BEEN A PRECONCERTED PLAN for a wholesale murder by Booth, Louis Payne, whose real name was Powell, George Atzerodt and probably as many as seven others. It was the purpose of the plotters to murder Lincoln, Grant, Johnson and Seward. Fortunately for Mr. Seward, he was in his own bed at home when Lewis Payne, who had been assigned to his murder, had managed to gain admission to the Seward home, after felling Frederick Seward with his revolver butt. He rushed into the bedroom of the Secretary of State, and attacked the ill man with a bowie knife, succeeding in slashing his cheek and stabbing him twice in the neck but did not manage to kill him. Fortunately the wire mesh bandage saved his throat from being fatally cut. Atzerodt had been assigned to the murder of Johnson. Possibly he ran out of liquor, for anyway his courage failed him and possibly he knew the record of Johnson's fearlessness and the attempt was not carried out. He had however taken a room at the Kirkwood House where Johnson was staying and had managed to get a room near Johnson.

Immediately after Lincoln drew his last breath, the Cabinet except Stanton, McCullough and Seward, met in the back parlor of the Petersen home and composed a letter to Johnson, advising him of Mr. Lincoln's death. To this Johnson replied that he would take the oath of office at ten o'clock that morning at the Kirkwood House, where he lived. There he received Chief Justice Chase, the members of the Cabinet and several Senators.

Eliza McArdle Johnson and her family were not in Washington, at this time. She had been driven from her residence in Greeneville in 1862 by the order of General E. Kirby Smith when that portion of Tennessee was occupied by the Confederates and soon thereafter the residence was used as barracks for soldiers. By that time her health had been broken and she was an invalid, but she and her family were given safe delivery behind the Confederate lines and so journeyed to Nashville. She later had returned to Greeneville. She had shared in all of her husband's sorrows but now she was too ill and too far away to share in his triumph.

In the parlor of the simple inn, the Kirkwood House, Andrew Johnson took the oath and became the seventeenth president of the United States.

Charles Francis Adams had once described him in 1861 as "a Southern Unionist, a poor white of Eastern Tennessee, who by native energy had elevated himself." Doubtless this was true, but he undoubtedly did not look it. Indeed he looked more the part of the aristocrat with his quiet, gentle and slightly formal manners. Thirty-nine years before he had driven his heavily ladened cart across the mountains to Greeneville and now at fifty-seven he took the oath as President. He probably could not have done it without the aid and encouragement of his Eliza and that fifteeenth day of April, 1865, was gray, gloomy and rainy. He had been successively tailor, alderman, mayor for two terms, member of the State Legislature, State Senator, Representative in the National House for five terms, Governor of his State for two terms, United States Senator, Military Governor of Tennessee and Brigadier General of volunteers, Vice-President and now President of the United States. Unlike Lincoln, he had seldom been defeated for office.

What must Eliza Johnson have felt? Perhaps she was too ill to think or worry too much about the responsibilities of her Andy. She was not there and did not come to Washington until some months later, in the summer.

There was no Atlantic cable and therefore the news was not received in England until twelve days later. Some days later

Sir Frederick Buell, Envoy Extraordinary of her Britannic Majesty, presented his credentials to the new President together with a message of condolence and sympathy from Queen Victoria. Seventy years before in 1795 Jacob Johnson, father of the President and a house carpenter by trade, had emigrated from Newcastle to Boston. That day from the reigning monarch had come a personal message to that brave pioneer. "It is with pleasure," said Sir Frederick, "that I convey the assurances of regard and good will which her Majesty entertains towards you, sir, the President of the United States." Andrew Johnson was not at a loss for words for his reply. Perhaps his mind went back to the days when he was a bound boy of Raleigh to Selby, a harsh taskmaster, and perhaps he said something of these thoughts to his Eliza, when she arrived, but there is no record of this. She was not nearly so conscious nor so defensive of plebeian birth as he.

His rewards had not been unaccompanied by grave sorrows. Johnson once in a speech before the Senate had said, "My wife and children have been turned into the street, and my house has been turned into a barracks, and for what? Because I stand by the Constitution? This is my offense. My sons have been imprisoned; my son-in-law has had to run to the mountains." Added to that later was the fact that his eldest son, Dr. Charles Johnson, a surgeon in the Union Army, had been killed in a fall from a horse in the Battle of Nashville. Not even Lincoln had to endure these hardships and heartaches, his wife and family were with him during the hard years from 1861 to 1865.

Funeral services for the assassinated president were held in the East Room of the White House on April 19, after which the body was removed to the rotunda of the Capitol. On the 21st it was started on its way to Springfield on the same route by which Lincoln had traveled four years before. In Philadelphia at Independence Hall, again at the City Hall in the City of New York and upon reaching Chicago, the body lay in state. At last on May 4, it was deposited in its final resting place at Springfield.

Immediately after Johnson had taken the oath of office he

sent a courteous note to Mrs. Lincoln, inviting her to stay on at the White House as long as she might desire to do so. Mr. Sam Hooper, a member of the House of Representatives, offered his comfortable house to Mr. Johnson. The house was situated at the corner of Fourteenth and H Streets. He used a room in the Treasury Department as an office, immediately adjoining and communicating with the office of Secretary of the Treasury Hugh McCullough. Mr. McCullough remembered that the President always arrived at his office before nine and usually stayed until five. He also remembered that Mr. Johnson was abstemious in food as well as in drink. There was never any liquor in his office and his luncheon usually consisted of a cup of tea and a cracker, and his office was open to everyone.

In front of the White House, a reviewing stand was erected and on May 22, the President reviewed Sherman's army. Washington was full to overflowing and the railroads were taxed to take care of the multitudes that came. Mrs. Lincoln was still living in the White House. General Sherman described it, thusly, "The signal gun was fired, when in person, attended by General Howard and all my staff, I rode slowly down Pennsylvania Avenue, the crowds of men, women, and children, densely lining the sidewalks, and almost obstructing the way. When I reached the Treasury Building and looked back, the sight was magnificent. The column was compact and the glittering muskets looked like a solid mass of steel moving with the regularity of a pendulum. It was in my judgment the most magnificent army in existence—sixty-five thousand men in splendid physique, who had just completed a march of nearly two thousand miles in a hostile country, in good drill, and who realized they were being closely scrutinized by thousands of their fellow countrymen and by foreigners."

At least one foreigner was duly impressed. The French Ambassador reported to Louis Napoleon and possibly his trans-Atlantic dreams of conquest were somewhat deflated, as well as that of his henchman, Maximilian. Perhaps he thought the Monroe Doctrine should be seriously read and considered.

It was a sight of beauty and grandeur but Andrew Johnson

could not have failed to remember that these same men had burned houses and despoiled plantations from Atlanta to the Carolinas and finally had rested in the town of Goldsboro, N. C. However General Sherman had shown a sense of decency and had spared the home in which a mother was expecting the birth of her baby. This baby, who later became Mrs. Robinson, wife of the owner and publisher of the Goldsboro *News-Argus*, is the authority for this statement. He had heeded a message sent to him.

Truly Sherman's definition: "War is Hell" could not be disputed. But Hell had now abated, or had it?

X : RECONSTRUCTION BEGINS

ONE WEEK LATER on May 29 Andrew Johnson took his first decisive step toward reconstruction and perhaps it was with a certain nostalgia that he chose to show his first act of generosity and amnesty toward his native state, though he never made this statement. His first reconstruction proclamation related only to North Carolina, but he had not intended to stop with this state.

"To the end . . . that the authority of the government of the United States may be restored and that peace, order and freedom be established, I, Andrew Johnson, President of the United States, do . . . hereby grant to all persons who have . . . participated in the existing rebellion, amnesty, and pardon with restoration of all rights of property except as to slaves. . . ." However fourteen groups were excepted from the benefits of this general amnesty. The thirteenth excluded all those who had "voluntarily participated in said rebellion and the estimated value of whose taxable property is over $20,000." For those thus, he declared "that special application may be made to the President for pardon by any person belonging to the excepted classes, and such clemency will be liberally extended as may be consistent with the facts of the case and the peace and dignity of the United States." Indeed this promise was fulfilled fully and wisely. This proclamation was in all essentials much like that of Lincoln issued on December 8, 1863, except that Lincoln's proclamation listed nothing resembling the thirteenth exception, involving a property disqualification. William W. Holden was appointed as Provisional Governor of the State of North Carolina.

Johnson found full authority for his proclamation to grant reprieves and pardons within his constitutional power as had Lincoln before him. Many historians have been unkind as well as false in their detractions. Blaine asserts, "He was not especially open to flattery, but it was noticed that words of commendation from his native section seemed peculiarly pleasing to him."

The proclamation further avowed that a person qualified as a voter for choosing delegates to the state convention must be a voter qualified as prescribed by the Constitution, and laws of the State of North Carolina in force immediately before the 20th day of May, A.D. 1861, the date of the so-called ordinance of secession. However the electors of the convention shall have previously taken the oath of amnesty as set forth in the President's proclamation of the same day. Thus North Carolina had the right to grant the franchise to her former slaves, if she desired to do so. It must have been indeed a satisfaction to Johnson to begin his work of reconstruction in the state in which he had been born and in which he had suffered so much. He had left North Carolina because he had been bound to a master and in no legal way had he been able to gain his release.

The Southern Negro particularly had a mind picture of Lincoln, not Johnson, as the deliverer from bondage. A Southern correspondent of the New York *Tribune* wrote the following account from Charleston, South Carolina the week following the assassination:

> I never saw such sad faces, or heard such heavy hearts beating, as here in Charleston. . . . The colored people . . . were like children bereaved of an only and loved parent. I saw one old woman going up the street wringing her hands and saying aloud,

as she walked looking straight ahead, so absorbed in her grief that she noticed no one,—

"O Lord. O Lord. O Lord. Massa Sam's dead. Massa Sam's dead, O Lord, Massa Sam's dead."

"Who's dead, Aunty?" she was asked.

"Massa Sam." she said, not looking at her enquirer—renewing her lamentations: "O Lord. O Lord. Lord. Massa Sam's dead."

"Who's Massa Sam?"

"Uncle Sam," she said. "O Lord. Lord."

"Who's Massa Sam, Aunty?"

"Massa Lincum." she answered, and resumed wringing her hands and moaning in utter hopelessness of sorrow. The poor creature was too ignorant to comprehend any difference between the very unreal Uncle Sam and the actual President; but her heart told her that he whom Heaven had sent in answer to her prayers was lying in a bloody grave, and she and her race were left—fatherless.

XI : ELIZA COMES TO WASHINGTON

Mrs. Lincoln had taken President Johnson at his word in the acceptance to remain in the White House as long as it suited her convenience. She remained there eight weeks, and so the President did not move until June 9. His health was none too good as he suffered from a kidney ailment. Also he had suffered a fracture of his right arm in a railroad accident and as surgery of the day did not afford the benefit of X-ray, the arm was allowed to heal not in complete alignment and for that reason writing was always difficult thereafter.

When, at long last, Eliza was able to join him in the White House, it was indeed a solace to him, though she could not do much in the way of the duties of the mistress of the White House. She occupied a room on the second floor, opposite the library, but she suffered the ravages of consumption for some years and there was no known treatment for the recovery of her disease in that era.

Martha Johnson Patterson, the President's eldest daughter,

had been carefully educated in "a young ladies' seminary." She was the wife of David T. Patterson and presided over the White House for her father. Martha Patterson had previously visited Washington during the administration of President Polk and knew the Blairs, the Lees and many other old families of Washington. She was a gracious and charming woman, which was coupled with dignity, good sense, clear judgment and executive ability. She was diplomatic and tactful. "We are plain people from the mountains of Tennessee," she calmly announced, "called here for a short time by a national calamity. I trust too much will not be expected of us."

She was one of the few mistresses of the White House who preferred to do some of the actual housekeeping, rather than trusting all to servants. She is said to have made the butter by hand, which was used by the presidential family, as well as some of the sewing. Mrs. Johnson passed most of her time sewing and crocheting, while she sat in a rocking chair, overlooking the White House lawn.

Both the President and his family were personally popular in Washington, as well they should have been! They had been long accustomed to political position for he had been twice Governor of Tennessee before the duties of Military Governor were thrust upon him.

Eliza McArdle Johnson was a constant invalid in her room across the hall from the President's library but the doors were always left ajar. It is said that her coughs, her sobs and sometimes her moans in the night would summon her husband to her bedside. The one available portrait of her at this time shows her to be a lovely lady, appearing far older than her fifty-five years, which was her age in 1865 when she came first to Washington. At this time, she parted her hair sedately in the middle and wore a white lace cap, together with a simple lace collar and large brooch, containing tresses under glass, according to the fashion of the day. It is needless to say that the hair in the brooch were the black locks of her beloved Andrew, whom she had married at seventeen.

She had lost one son, Charles, during the War, but she still had her two daughters, Martha and Mary, her second son, Robert, and the baby of them all, young Andrew. Mary had married Colonel Daniel Stover of the Union Army. Both Mary Stover and Martha were well educated, poised and attractive young matrons at this time. The latter was thirty-seven years old when she became mistress of the White House and was the mother of young children. The Stovers also had children, so during this administration the White House was enlivened by their activities. One granddaughter, Lillie Stover, was especially dear to the President's heart.

Secretary of the Treasury McCullough made the remark that, "More sensible or unpretending women never occupied the White House than Mrs. Johnson and her daughters." Mrs. Lincoln had had a dressmaker, a former slave, Elizabeth Keckley, who after once carrying some completed work to the White House during the Johnson Administration, found Mrs. Patterson busily sewing and said that she could not recall having ever seen Mrs. Lincoln with a needle in her hand. However, Mrs. Keckley for some reason was not especially impressed with new White House mistress for whom she made some elaborate frocks.

Some of Washington's so-called high society felt inclined to patronize the President's family, but their success was poor indeed. Mrs. Patterson never allowed her patronizing callers to forget for an instant that she was the daughter of the President and that she needed no aid and took small interest in snobs. Washington society and the people in general were highly pleased by the dignity and demeanor of the President's family.

Senator Doolittle commented on the fact that Mrs. Patterson was a model hostess and mistress of the White House and had a charming and gracious manner at state dinners.

The President's brother, William, had now moved to Texas. He wrote asking the President for an important appointment. However, Mr. Johnson sent him $1000 and advised him to live frugally, adding that when this amount was gone, he would send him more. William wrote with thanks, but insisted that it was an office, not money that he desired. The President again replied that he was opposed to appointing relatives to office. William continued to write and ask for a United States Marshal's job in Texas. The President relented, remarking to Benjamin Truman, his secretary, "That isn't much. Better to give it to him, hadn't I?" It is to be remembered that this is the same older brother, who did nothing to aid young Andrew, when it was necessary for the seventeen-year-old boy to undertake the support of his mother.

Another incident of personal importance happened that summer. A group of New York bankers and merchants subscribed monies to buy the President a handsome carriage and span of horses. Johnson politely refused the gift with courteous words of refusal, which was met with wholesale approval by the entire country. When this equipage was sold at public auction, it only brought half the price of $6,000 that was paid for it.

During this period Mr. Johnson on one occasion caused a basket of flour to be sent from a mill which he owned in Greeneville. The basket was left in his bedroom overnight for some reason. While he was preparing for bed, he noticed some mice playing around and nibbling the flour, so he placed the basket on the hearth, in order to allow them to get their fill undisturbed during the night.

After the reunion with his family, he often took long walks in Rock Creek Park or drives to Silver Spring. The children would take off their shoes and stockings and wade in the brook. On one of these occasions, while returning from Silver Spring, a thunder shower came up suddenly. The President saw a poor woman on the roadside, ragged and dripping wet, walking to town with a baby in her arms. He had his carriage stopped, the woman was invited to occupy the seat opposite him and was taken safely to her home.

Robert Johnson, the oldest surviving son, was now thirty-one-years old and a colonel in the army. He assisted his father as a secretary. There were twelve members of the family: the

President; his beloved and now invalided wife, Eliza; the two daughters, Mrs. Patterson and Mrs. Stover; the two sons, Robert and Andrew, Jr., now thirteen; Senator Patterson; as well as five grandchildren.

One of the White House workers during this administration, described the White House as resembling "an old fashioned, hospitable, home-like farm house." What more could a democratic people have desired? At the same time General Sherman described the City of Washington in a letter to his wife: "Washington is as corrupt as Hell, made so by the looseness and extravagance of war. I will avoid it as a pest house."

Mrs. Johnson during her sojourn in the White House was so much of an invalid that few knew her outside of intimate family friends. Her influence, however, was a strong one with the President and it was exerted in the direction of toleration. A slight movement of her hands with a touch on her husband's arm and a "Now, Andrew," made it easy to see that the woman who had taught him to write and had helped him through his struggling youth and had read to him through long winter evenings so that his active mind might develop while he plied his tailoring trade, still held a steadying influence in his life.

She was a sweet-faced woman with traces of beauty along the sharpened lines of her thinning face. Her life in Washington was not a happy time for her. She once told Colonel William Crook, bodyguard of the President and a man who was always friendly and attentive to the invalided lady, "I was far more content and happy when Andrew was an industrious young tailor in Greeneville."

Together the Johnsons had planned and later sent, during the administration of Polk, their eldest daughter, Martha, to a school in Georgetown to be educated. Since her father was by then in the House of Representatives, Martha had frequently been a guest at the White House. Therefore Martha Johnson was not unversed in social graces and presided with a cultivated exactness in the discharge of social duties as mistress of the White House. She and her father understood the value and place of social functions, both from his training as Governor of Tennessee and her familiarity with Washington official life. She was an intimate friend of the family of old Francis Blair dating from her Georgetown school days.

XII : JOHN WILKES BOOTH

MANY YEARS AFTER THE TRAGEDY of Lincoln's assassination, Sir Charles Wyndham, a noted Englishman, spoke of Booth as "one of the few to whom that ill-used term of genius might be applied with perfect truth." Booth was handsome with an ascetic face, high forehead, full lips, sweeping black hair, perfect proportions of figure and brilliant eyes. He had been born in Maryland, of a well known actor family and went on the stage as a lad. He had by 1865 become well known as a popular actor, especially in the South. As the Confederate fortunes faded, his heart grew furious with anger and doubtless something in his emotional brain snapped. He must have brooded over the wrongs of his beloved South until finally he conceived the plot of kidnapping Lincoln; carrying him across the Potomac into Confederate territory, through the lines of both armies and either holding him in prison or holding him for ransom. As early as January 1864, a definite plan had been formulated.

Booth realized that it would be impossible for him to carry through such an ambitious plot without assistance. Therefore he tried to enlist the aid of others who were willing and anxious to risk all for the Confederate cause. His fellow conspirators in the plot were two former schoolmates, O'Laughlin and Arnold, as well as another actor, by the name of Chester. On one wintry night Lincoln supposedly was to attend a performance at Ford's Theater, but on account of the very bad weather, he did not go. Later Booth learned of a Confederate agent, one John Surratt, and began to cultivate his friendship. He overdid this to such an extent that Surratt began to be suspicious. Finally,

Booth did reveal his plan to Surratt, and in true theatrical fashion, he peered under the bed, looked into the wardrobe, and crept up to Surratt, and whispered, "We must be careful, even the walls have ears." Then he hesitated a moment, adding, "It is to kidnap President Lincoln and carry him off to Richmond."

Surratt at first thought the undertaking thoroughly foolhardy. He relented a few days later, and admitted that it might be possible to take the President across the Potomac by the famous underground railroad and get him through the lines of the two armies. He himself was willing to do anything for the Confederate cause. If the plan had been carried out in 1864 as originally planned, it is possible that the President might have been used as a hostage to be exchanged for thousands of Confederate soldiers and the end of the war might have been considerably postponed.

However the lack of opportunity prevented the culmination of the kidnapping plan. But on March 16, 1865, Lincoln was announced to plan to attend a benefit performance of *Still Waters Run Deep* to be given at the Soldiers' Home. Booth's kidnapping group was well organized and within less than an hour, he had seven mounted men, armed and waiting to overpower Mr. Lincoln as he drove to Soldiers' Home. Again Providence intervened. On account of the pressure of business, someone else was sent to represent Mr. Lincoln and when the waiting henchmen peered into the Presidential carriage, instead of Lincoln, a stranger looked out at them. At once being suspicious and frightened, they thought that the plot had been discovered and the stranger was placed in Lincoln's place as a decoy. The plotters scattered. But Booth, through his personal charm and magnetism, again gathered several of his co-conspirators together. Booth and the half-drunken Lewis Payne, were together on the night of April 11 when Mr. Lincoln made his speech announcing Lee's Surrender to a rejoicing throng by the light of a candle. Some reference was made to the fact that those Negroes who were more intelligent and those who had borne arms for the Union might be accorded the voting privilege. This talk "of giving votes to niggers" so infuriated the two men that, as they walked away, Booth said to Payne, "This is the last speech that he will ever make."

Booth called for his mail at Ford's Theater on the afternoon of April 14 and learned that Lincoln would attend the performance that night. The kidnapping plan had now been abandoned and a detailed plan of assassination had been formulated after April 11.

On the afternoon of April 14, Booth called all his conspirators for a conference at his room at the Herndon House to assign definitely the part each would play. Atzerodt, to whom the assassination of Johnson had been assigned, definitely refused, saying that he went into the plot as a kidnapping, but that he would not kill. Booth told him that he was a fool, for he would hang anyway and with that they parted. Booth, later in the afternoon, made an attempt to contact William A. Browning, Johnson's secretary, whom Booth had known when he played in Nashville before the War, but was unable to locate Browning. Atzerodt had earlier, on April 12, asked Colonel W. R. Nevin to point out the Vice-President to him and so had sized him up. On April 14, Atzerodt had registered at the Kirkwood House, where Johnson was registered and had been assigned, by request, to Room 126. In order to reach his room, he had to pass Andrew Johnson's room. But after the last meeting with Booth on the afternoon of April 14, Atzerodt went from barroom to barroom drinking with anyone who offered him a drink. His courage had failed him but later this did not save his neck.

Doubtless John Wilkes Booth believed that he was truly a Southern hero. After the dramatic shooting, he fled to southern Maryland, having broken his leg in his jump from the stage of Ford's Theater.

At some previous date Booth had known of the location of the residence of a young Dr. Mudd through the purchase of a horse. He could not have known that he would need the services of a physician on this night. On the night of April 14, Booth in true theatrical style, had disguised himself with a beard, and as Dr. Mudd had only seen him once he did not recognize the wounded man, who claimed that he had injured his leg in a fall from his horse. When Booth and his companion, Herold, called at the Mudd residence in the middle of the night, it is not puzzling that Dr. Mudd did not recognize the man who was a most casual acquaintance.

Michael O'Laughlin was arrested in Baltimore, and Samuel Arnold at Fortress Monroe. Atzerodt, still drunk, was arrested in western Maryland but Booth was not shot, while resisting capture, until April 26, in company with another conspirator, Herold. Weichman turned informer and included Mrs. Mary E. Surratt, mother of John Surratt, in the plot. Although $25,000 was offered as a reward for the capture of John Surratt, by Secretary Stanton, he escaped for several years. He had had experience as a Confederate agent, and was more skilled in methods of escape.

Richard Montgomery and Sanford Conover presented themselves to Stanton, claiming to have been employed by the Confederate States in 1864 in Canada and said that they had access to certain secrets there. They made several trips to Canada, claiming each time they returned that they had "positive proof" that Jefferson Davis had engineered the assassination plot. Under the direction of Secretary Stanton, everyone who was captured was put under pressure to implicate the Confederate leaders in the plot.

Previously the relationship between Andrew Johnson and his War Secretary, Mr. Stanton, had been very warm and friendly. It is not to be wondered at, that at this time the investigations of Secretary Stanton were relied upon as valid and correct. It is to be admitted that punishment was a favorite theme of the President. Again and again he had declared that he desired amnesty for the misguided followers of the Secession but that hanging was too good for conscious traitors.

Andrew Johnson sincerely loved Abraham Lincoln and his murder had moved him intensely. Stanton claimed that there were positive proofs of the complicity of Davis in this murder and that Washington was a hotbed of Secession sympathizers. He insisted that a civil jury would never convict the conspirators and Johnson listened with a believing ear.

The President consulted with the Attorney General, asking an opinion as to the proper mode of trial. James Speed was Attorney General in Lincoln's Cabinet and also in Johnson's. His brother, Joshua, had been one of Lincoln's friends back in Springfield, Illinois, when an awkward lawyer had shown up friendless, with a few articles of clothing and three law books. It was this same Joshua, who had introduced Lincoln to Mary Todd and later had brought Mr. Lincoln to the parental Speed home in Louisville to recover from that unfortunate New Year's Day in 1841 when Lincoln failed to appear at his own wedding. James Speed at first seemed to approve a civil trial but, he too, was later influenced by the bitter vehemence of the War Secretary and submitted a legal opinion to the President, mentioning the disturbed state of the country at this time, when the War had not been formally proclaimed to be at an end. He recommended that a military commission be formed to try the conspirators which was the aim of Stanton in detail.

Two weeks of fevered discussions followed, at the end of which the Bureau of Military Justice announced that it was ready to present proof of its charges. On May 1, the President ordered a military commission to be set up to try all of the conspirators. He stated that the Attorney General had given him his opinion that the trial should be before such a commission and he ordered nine competent military officers to be designated to serve. Joseph Holt was Judge Advocate of the War Department and as such was the head of the Bureau of Military Justice. In 1864 Holt had been mentioned as Lincoln's running mate. Now he had become a rabid Radical and a willing tool in Stanton's hands to wreak vengeance on guilty and innocent alike. They were aided by Colonel Burnett, who was experienced in influencing military commissions to impose death penalties. Now Stanton wrote Holt that the President wished to be furnished with a list of persons, lately in Canada and Richmond, against whom there was evidence of complicity in the assassination. The list was sent immediately.

Later in the day when the Cabinet met, Stanton produced his list, which enumerated Jefferson Davis, Jacob Thompson, George N. Sanders and other Confederate civil officers as instigators of the plot. Then Stanton urged the President to issue a proclamation to offer generous rewards for the capture and arrest of these Confederate officers. The Cabinet officers agreed with Stanton and that afternoon the proclamation was issued, for the following: Jefferson Davis, Jacob Thompson, Beverly Tucker, Clement Clay, George N. Sanders, William N. Cleary and other traitors against the United States who were, at that time, harbored in Canada. The rewards were as follows: for Davis, $100,000; for each of the others, $25,000, with the exception of that for Cleary, Clay's clerk, for whom the amount was set at $10,000.

On May 4, Beverly Tucker and George N. Sanders addressed a letter to Johnson from Montreal, stating that these charges were "a living, burning lie, known to be such by yourself and all your surrounders." They denied that they had ever seen Booth or that he had ever sent them a note or sought an interview with them. They challenged the President to name any nine of twenty-five Federal Generals, whom they named, to form a court martial trial.

These things happened even before Lincoln was buried for the funeral actually took place in Springfield on May 4. However the military commission was formally appointed by the Adjutant General on May 6 and ordered to meet for trial on May 8, but actually met on May 9, just one month after the surrender at Appomattox by Lee to Grant.

XIII : MRS. MARY SURRATT

THE OLD PENITENTIARY was the site of the meeting of the military commission on that May morning. Arrayed in full dress uniform, the nine officers of the court appeared. Major General David Hunter was the President of the Commission. It was he who had sat at the head of Lincoln's coffin as the funeral cortege had gone, so recently, from place to place on the route to Springfield. Also he was a Radical, as were the other eight members of the Commission, and he had commanded a regiment of Negro troops.

The military court of 1865 was strangely organized as a court of justice. No real judge presided, but instead a Judge Advocate, who both prosecuted the accused and also determined the law of the court. It was the same as if today the district attorney in a civil court also sat as the judge on the bench. But Stanton's idea was not to administer justice but to convict the accused. The prosecution was represented by Judge Holt, Colonel Burnett and John A. Bingham, as vindictive and brow-beating attorneys as could be obtained.

Into this first full session of the commission were brought eight prisoners, one of whom was a woman. All were chained, and the chains clanked with every step. Also heavy handcuffs were on the men. Mrs. Surratt did not wear these wristlets but iron anklets were on her feet.

Briefly Mrs. Surratt's connection with the case seemed to be chiefly that she was John Surratt's mother and he had not been apprehended. She had previously owned an inn at Surrattville, in Maryland, about twelve miles from Washington and in October, before the assassination, she had opened a boarding-house in Washington proper. Some of the conspirators had boarded with her. Booth had not. He had lived at the National Hotel and at a later date had a room at the Herndon House. A man named John M. Lloyd was keeping her Surrattville tavern and another witness against her was Lewis Weichman, who boarded with her. Although he stated that she "had been a mother to me," he testified against her and was the first person to connect her with the case. These two men were frightened for their own necks and so turned state's evidence. Weichman was a government clerk. John Surratt, Atzerodt, and Herold had gotten Lloyd to hide two carbines and a long rope for them out at Surrattville about six weeks before the assassination and there was nothing that proved he was unwilling to do so. At the trial Lloyd stated that Mrs. Surratt on the afternoon of April 14 had driven out to the tavern and had told him "to get the shooting irons ready." But remember the date for the assassination was not set until sometime during the afternoon of April 14 and the tavern was twelve miles distant, which in those days of bad roads would have been nearly three hours drive. However no one seemed to calculate that. Though it was proven that on the afternoon of April 14, Lloyd was so drunk that he would have been incapable of remembering what might have been said to him, his testimony was accepted as credible. Mrs. Surratt was able to prove that she went out to the tavern in order to collect some money from a man who had bought 75 acres of her Maryland farm. Before the trial a government detective had stated that Lloyd had not mentioned Mrs. Surratt, when arrested, but at the trial, he said on the witness sand, "Undoubtedly, I lied there. . . . It is part of my business." This seemed to be a part of a great many people's business in higher places than this man.

Weichman was a clerk in the War Department and a schoolmate of John Surratt and had boarded with Mrs. Surratt from the time she had opened the boardinghouse in Washington. He had also known Booth, Atzerodt, and Lewis Payne quite well. It seemed that Weichman had borrowed a buggy from Booth to take Mrs. Surratt out to her country tavern. He testified that on one occasion Booth had called on Mrs. Surratt, but as far as anyone knew this was the only time she had ever seen the slayer and Weichman was trying to save himself by implicating someone else when he made this doubtful claim. The only other item of so-called evidence against Mrs. Surratt was an occurrence on the night of April 17. On this occasion troops had come to the house of Mrs. Surratt, arresting her daughter, Anna, and herself, and were preparing to take them to prison. A roughly-dressed man, with pantaloons rolled up over the tops of his heavy boots, a pickaxe in his hand and a gray shirt sleeve over his head for a cap, was seen there by the troops.

They inquired what he wanted and he stated that he had been employed by the landlady to dig a gutter and had come to find out where it was to be dug on the following morning. Investigation by them proved this man to be Lewis Payne but when Mrs. Surratt was brought face to face with the man so attired and asked if she knew the man, she replied, "Before God, sir, I do not know this man and have never seen him and I did not hire him to dig a gutter for me." This was in the dim lamplight before the days of electric lights, but this was taken as incriminating evidence.

The officer who had taken the articles from the dead body of Booth was not questioned as to exactly what they were. No diary was shown or even mentioned and no one seemed to know anything of the existence of one. There was a diary and at this time it was in the hands of Secretary Stanton and it showed in detail that the plan was originally one of kidnapping, not murder. It is highly improbable that any of the conspirators except Booth, Payne and Atzerodt knew anything of a plan of assassination.

The case of Dr. Mudd was really worse than that of Mrs. Surratt, for he did not even know any of the conspirators, except that he had seen Booth on one occasion by chance during the purchase of a horse. He treated Booth for a leg injury in the middle of the night, when Booth and Herold came to the Mudd home in southern Maryland, but no doctor who has taken the Hippocratic oath could have done less. He did not even know that Lincoln had been shot and certainly his callers did not tell him. Yet he was sentenced to life imprisonment and except for the fact that he aided in the treatment of his fellow prisoners in an epidemic of yellow fever some three years later, he would have spent the rest of his life in prison. Prior to this time he had been forced to work on a rock pile with his legs encased in chains. He was pardoned by President Johnson before the end of his administration for his medical services.

But for Mrs. Surratt there was no reprieve. The commission sentenced the prisoners in this order: Herold, who was with Booth when the latter was shot; Atzerodt, whose courage failed him when it was time for him to murder Johnson; and Payne, who attempted to murder Secretary of State Seward while he lay in his sick bed. These three were sentenced to death by hanging. The commission probably thought Mrs. Surratt guilty for the three Judge Advocates were allowed to sit in on the secret sessions and urge the death penalty and all three were bloodthirsty. It was necessary for two-thirds of the commission to vote for the death sentence if it was to be imposed.

After the first day's sentencing, five of the nine officers had expressed themselves as unwilling to impose the death sentence on Mrs. Surratt. They had the full right to extend mercy. Holt reported the disagreement to Stanton and he immediately conferred with Bingham and Holt and a scheme was devised by the three. As five of the commission were unwilling to condemn the woman by hanging, the prosecutors, Bingham, Holt and Burnett, might suggest to the nine commissioners that she be condemned formally and then the members who dissented could later petition the President to commute her sentence to imprisonment. Holt made a bloodthirsty speech, denouncing the women of the South, pleading that Mrs. Surratt be made an example and one of the five gave in but four were unwilling to sentence her to death. Another argument was that John Surratt would not let his mother be hanged but would come out of his place of hiding to save her. This brought one more vote against her and only three were left to have any feeling of mercy.

Under military law all court martial sentences must be reviewed by the President. This was left to Judge Holt as President of the Bureau of Military Justice. He had been the hero of a hundred court martials before. This was on the last day of June when the commission adjourned.

Andrew Johnson was ill at the time. He suffered excruciatingly from sand and gravel attacks due to his kidney ailment and at this time was in bed. He had held no Cabinet meeting for more than a week, but on Wednesday, July 5, he was able to sit up. Sometime that day Judge Holt started to the White House but did not take the mass of testimony with him. He took only a brief extract and a report of the proceedings which he had prepared, together with the commission's findings and the sentence. General Mussey was the secretary who admitted Holt to see Johnson on that day. The President remarked to Mussey that he was going to look over the findings with Holt and could see no one. Two or three hours later Holt came out and Mussey questioned the President as to his approval. He was told that he had ordered the sentences, where it was death, to be carried out on the Friday following. He added that he did not want to see anyone on "errands of mercy." He must have been indeed a sick man on that day.

Milton's *The Age of Hate* is the authority for making the following statement from pages 207 and 208. He states that in April 1929 he examined the original documents of these findings wrapped in a crumbling piece of brown paper under the eaves of the State, War and Navy Building.

The findings and sentences of the commission are written upon a few sheets of legal cap, obviously at one time fastened together at the top, for there are several holes punched through them for the insertion of binding ribbons or tape. The pages are now numbered in pencil. On the 16th page thus numbered, comes the entry of the adjournment of the commission. On the same page, half way down, begins the presidential indorsement. The body of the indorsement is not in the handwriting of Andrew Johnson, but in that of Joseph Holt. It is continued over on the back of the page, which is numbered 17, and is signed, in a distinctly different hand and in ink of a different color, "Andrew Johnson, Pres."

The recommendation for mercy is to be found in the file immediately following, not preceding, the page telling of the adjournment and bearing Johnson's indorsement. The recommendation is penciled 18. It is on a different kind of paper, a double foolscap page, hinged at the top. The papers as a whole are pierced by three holes at about the center of the top margin, obviously for the insertion of binding ribbons. At this point on the pages of the petition for clemency the paper is torn out; the tear is a very old one, that might have well have been caused by jerking this petition from the general file. The physical evidence justifies the suspicion that, before Holt submitted the findings of the court to President Johnson, he detached the petition for clemency from the file, and returned it to its place after he had won his end.

At noon on Thursday, July 6, the order of sentencing was read to Mrs. Surratt. None of the three dissenting members of the commission had called on the President to personally recommend mercy. Certainly John Surratt had been given short opportunity to hear of the sentencing of his mother. Indeed it was to be seen later that he was not even in the confines of the United States at the time; but even if he had been, no time was allowed for him to give himself up in an effort to save his mother. When the sentence of hanging was read to Mary Surratt, she protested her innocence in faltering and tearful words. She pleaded for a few more days to prepare herself for the grave. She seemed in danger of insanity and physicians were summoned to keep her sane, but it was only an empty gesture. Her daughter, Anna, stood on the street outside the grim prison walls and cried out in grief and anguish. The tight-lipped guards replied with utter silence, but what else could they do?

As a last resort Anna Surratt made a last personal appeal. She managed to enter the White House and attempted to mount the stairs, leading to the President's office on the second floor. When she tried to gain entrance in this fashion, she was prevented by Senator Lane of Kansas and Preston King. She lay down on the bottom step and sobbed out her grief. Mrs. Martha Johnson Patterson saw her there and stooped to comfort her, saying "My poor dear, you break my heart, but there is not a thing I can do."

As a further last resort, friends of Mrs. Surratt, appealed to the civil courts. The Constitution of the United States contains the safeguard of the writ of habeas corpus. On Friday morning, July 7 a Judge Wylie of the civil courts, issued a writ, which was served on General Hancock. At 11:30 that same morning General Hancock appeared before this Judge to make a return. This return certified that the writ of habeas corpus had been suspended by order of the President, and annexed to his return was a copy of this order dated at 10 o'clock that same morning of the execution directing General Hancock to proceed with the execution of Mrs. Surratt.

At five o'clock that Friday morning, three days after Independence Day, Mrs. Surratt had been removed to a solitary cell on the main floor of the penitentiary in order to provide the first step to the gallows. Many residents of Washington, relatives, friends and many who knew this unfortunate woman not at all, flocked around the White House that morning. They doubted the guilt of the woman, but none of them saw the President. He had said, "I can see no one on this business. Let them see Judge Holt and if there is anything new, tell him."

In this multitude of seekers after mercy, was the widow of Stephen A. Douglas, who had debated with Abraham Lincoln. She was in the White House at the time and came down from the second floor weeping bitterly. Priests who had testified as to the character of Mrs. Surratt at the trial sought admission to see the President but they were refused.

The bells tolled that day, as well they might and soldiers tramped through the Washington streets. In the execution yard were four scaffolds below which were four chairs. Flags were flying and in full sight there were four open graves and four coffins. There was a steady rain to such an extent that an aide found it necessary to hold an umbrella over General Hartranft for him to read the sentence to the prisoners.

The death march began. Mrs. Surratt, dressed in black, with bonnet and veil, was supported by two bareheaded priests as well as two soldiers for she was too infirm to walk. Lewis Payne walked behind her, and in a last outburst, in rapid words he cried out a confession, clearing her of all complicity, especially in regard to his claim that she had employed him to dig a gutter for her on April 18. Immediately behind him came Atzerodt and Herold also to be hanged. Four others, Dr. Mudd, O'Laughlin, Arnold and Spangler were given prison sentences. Spangler received the shortest sentence of six years.

Mary Surratt was practically unconscious when the noose was placed around her neck, as she sat in the chair below the gallows prepared for her. A hood was drawn over her face, a signal was given and the scaffold fell. In a few moments her body, as well as the other three executed with her, ceased to writhe and both justice and vengeance had been done.

A prison physician pronounced them all dead, they were cut down and the bodies were laid on the tops of the coffins. Hasty autopsies were made at about four o'clock that afternoon and the burials were made side by side in the prison yard. There was a flourish of trumpets and a beat of drums, as the executioners marched away. Their duty was complete.

It was not until 1867 that John Surratt was apprehended and tried. At that time Andrew Johnson claimed vehemently that no recommendation for mercy, for a commutation of punishment for Mrs. Surratt was ever submitted or mentioned to him. He sent for the file and examined it and saw that the petition was now attached in such a way as to show that this was done at a later date. On at least one occasion he was heckled by members of an audience in a political speech with cries of "Tell us about Mrs. Surratt." This happened when he made a series of speeches in his well known "swing around the circle."

Toward the close of Mr. Johnson's administration there was a tragic aftermath, when Edwin Booth, John Wilkes Booth's noble brother, made a request for the possession of the body of the murderer, which up to this time had been lying in an unmarked grave at the Arsenal. With no spirit of bitterness, but with deep sadness, he requested permission to remove the body of his brother and the request was granted. The family buried the body in their plot.

XIV : JEFFERSON DAVIS AND CLEMENT CLAY

ELEVEN DAYS AFTER MRS. SURRATT was hung, the President discussed the case of Jefferson Davis with the Cabinet members and wisely decided that the former President of the Confederacy and others accused of treason with him should be tried by the civil courts. John Surratt had fled to Canada and from there had escaped to England, but this fact was still unknown in the States.

Davis was captured on May 10, 1865 by James Wilson's cavalry. He was informed that he was charged with being the brain behind the murder of President Lincoln. Davis, in order to show his intense dislike for Andrew Johnson made the statement that Johnson should indeed know the falsity of this charge for he certainly knew that he (Davis) preferred Lincoln to him. The charge had originated in the Bureau of Military Justice and Johnson did not know that it was untrue. He had served in the United States Senate with Davis.

Jefferson Davis and Clement C. Clay were placed in the casements at Fortress Monroe. They were were put in inner rooms with the windows heavily barred and the outer rooms were guarded by two sentries. They were locked in with a heavy key, which was kept by the general officer of the guard. Outside there was a long line of sentries, with another line at the top of the parapet overhead, and a third line across the moats upon the counterscarp. Even today there is no more dismal place than the casement in which Mr. Davis was imprisoned. A lamp was kept burning day and night in the prisoners' rooms.

Furthermore at Stanton's instigation General Miles put Davis in irons with riveted and padlocked fetters on his legs. This was done to prevent his running in case of escape, according to General Miles. However when President Johnson heard of this treatment to Mr. Davis, he sent Hugh McCullough, Secretary of the Treasury, to investigate with this statement, "Davis was the head devil among the traitors, and he ought to be hung; but he should have a fair trial and not be brutally treated while a prisoner." While Davis and Johnson served in the Senate together, prior to 1861, it is a generally accepted fact by historians that they did not like each other. While still in prison Mr. Davis in a conversation with Dr. Craven, the kindly prison physician, had said of Mr. Johnson, "The position of Mr. Johnson with his associates in the South, has never been pleasant, not from any fault or superciliousness on their side, but solely due to the intense, almost morbidly sensitive pride of Mr. Johnson. Sitting with associates, many of whom he knew pretended to aristocracy, Mr. Johnson seemed to set his own mind, and keep ever present with him, his democratic or plebeian origin as a bar to social relation."

However before the War, the South as well as the North was ready to heap honors on this Tennessee mountaineer, who was half English and half Scotch-Irish in origin. Here was an extremely attractive man, magnetic, meticulously dressed, but who apparently could not win the lasting affection of the masses as the awkward, as well as homely man, Abraham Lincoln did.

However, this man, Andrew Johnson permitted Mrs. Jefferson Davis, when she wrote to him from Montreal with the request to be permitted to come to see her husband, to be allowed this privilege.

When Secretary McCullough paid a visit to Mr. Davis at Fortress Monroe at the President's request, he found the Confederate President pacing the ramparts in the company of two soldiers. McCullough described him as a brave and high-bred gentleman, who could not demean himself as a criminal. Only on direct questioning did Mr. Davis tell of the barbarous treatment he had received. He had been allowed no newspapers or books, except a book on military tactics, which could scarcely have interested him. Davis added that at this time he was permitted a daily walk and stated that his present quarters were such of which a prisoner charged with high treason should not complain.

The so-called evidence against Davis and Clay was supplied by Sanford Conover and two other rascals by the names of

Campbell and Snevel. They claimed that they were actually present with John Surratt in the spring of 1865 at an interview between Jefferson Davis and Judah Benjamin when the murder of Lincoln was plotted. A year later in May 1866, Campbell admitted that his deposition accusing Jefferson Davis was a fabrication of lies, written out for him by Conover. He had committed them to memory and received $625 and for his lies, Snevel received only $475. Conover was present when these confessions were made. He was then permitted to go to New York City in the custody of a Sergeant-at-Arms to search for other witnesses. In some way upon their arrival in New York, Conover managed to elude the officer and escaped.

However this did not prevent a report from the judiciary committee that charged Jefferson Davis as not only guilty of treason but also of complicity in the murder of Lincoln. Nothing further was done to take steps to formally accuse him of this crime.

It is possible that Johnson was remembering Mr. Lincoln's story which was told to a party of gentlemen, who had anxiously asked, "What will you do with Jeff Davis when the Confederacy falls . . ."

To this Lincoln replied, "There was a boy in Springfield, who saved his money and bought a coon, which after the novelty wore off, became a great nuisance. He was one day leading him through the streets and had his hands full to keep clear of the little vixen who had torn his clothes half off of him. At length he sat down on the curbstone, completely fagged out. A man passing was stopped by the lad's disconsolate expression and asked the matter. 'Oh,' was the lad's reply, 'the coon is such a trouble to me.' 'Why don't you get rid of him?' 'Hush' said the boy, 'don't you see he is gnawing his rope off. I am going to let him do it and then I will go home and tell the folks that he got away from me.'"

Mrs. Clement C. Clay, wife of the Senator from Alabama, came to Washington in February 1866, and called on President Johnson several times in hope of gaining some clemency for her husband, who was then in the casements at Fortress Monroe. Judge Holt hated Davis and Clay because Holt had originally espoused the Southern cause, but later became a Union man. He had been born in Kentucky but at an early age had moved to Mississippi, where he had known Davis well. Holt had filed in the War Department a report on the case of C. C. Clay, Jr. Mrs. Clay had written to Holt, requesting that she be allowed to see this report. Her letter was not answered. She went to Washington in hopes of getting an opportunity of seeing this report. It happened that she called to see Mr. Johnson on a day that he had the official copy of this report in his office. She asked the assistance of the President in seeing a copy of this report. On a promise of complete secrecy he allowed her to take the original copy and to copy such excerpts as she felt would aid her.

It is to be remembered that Joseph Holt had been Clement Clay's friend in the days when they knew each other before the War and yet in this report Holt wrote that his guilt was relieved of all improbability by his previous history and criminal surroundings. One wonders if Holt considered the fact that he had been a part of this previous history.

Mrs. Clay returned this official copy of the report to Mr. Johnson and understandably was intensely alarmed about the future of her husband. She told Mr. Johnson that she had been informed that he had refused to allow a military court composed of Holt, Speed and Secretary Stanton try Mr. Davis and her husband. The President assured her that this was true. She entreated him to give her his solemn oath that so long as he was the President that he would never allow these two innocent men to be tried by that bloodthirsty military commission. Mr. Johnson answered: "I promise, Mrs. Clay; trust me." "I will; I do," she answered.

Johnson made good his promise to her. If Johnson hated all so-called aristocrats as his detractors have claimed, it is strange that he did not take this excellent opportunity to gain revenge on these two men so representative of the old South at this time. There must have been something very forgiving in his heart for the helpless.

Mr. Johnson gave Mrs. Clay a permit to visit her husband at Fortress Monroe. This was in December 1865 and in some way she managed to arrive at the casements about breakfast time. General Miles, having benefited by the tutelage under Stanton, did not allow her to see Mr. Clay until late afternoon. As soon as she returned to Washington, she went to see Mr. Johnson and he received her quietly and graciously. Naturally she was indignant and she began her conversation thusly, "Mr. Johnson, who is the President of the United States?" "I am supposed to be," he answered and shrugged his shoulders. She then explained in detail that his signed letter was not honored for many hours and that she waited nearly all day for General Miles' permission to see her husband, while the wires were held by the Secretary of War in order to prevent her from communicating with the President.

Some two months later in February 1866, she begged Johnson to release Clay and Davis. The President replied that it was the wisest policy to hold them a little longer to satisfy the public clamor; Mr. Stanton had just left the White House, ". . . clamoring for the blood of Davis and Clay." Stanton had bowed to her as he passed her in the corridor. It is to be remembered that the same commission of the Bureau of Military Justice that had tried Mrs. Surratt had found Jefferson Davis and Clement C. Clay guilty of conspiracy in the murder of Mr. Lincoln and except for the intervention of Johnson the same commission would have sat on trial for them.

It was not until the May term of the United States District Court of Virginia in 1866, nearly a year later, that Davis was at last indicted. Davis had expressed himself as hoping for a speedy trial, but when the President inquired of Chief Justice Chase if he could hold a term of the Circuit Court in Virginia in the fall of 1865, Mr. Chase declined to do so. Therefore Davis spent the winter of 1865 and 1866 in the casements at Fortress Monroe.

Time dragged on until on May 4, 1867, when there was a new commander at Fortress Monroe, General Burton. As Jefferson Davis had not been tried and approximately two years had passed since his arrest, his friends determined to bring him into court through a writ of habeas corpus. An order was issued by the President for General Burton to surrender Jefferson Davis upon any process which might issue from a Federal Court in the State of Virginia. On May 7 a small steamer left the Fortress with the former president of the Confederacy and his wife, Varina Davis. About sunset the steamer reached Richmond. A crowd had gathered, but opened to let their former President pass through. As he passed through the avenue thus made, many reached out a hand and touched his coat. On May 13 in the Confederate Building in Richmond on the second floor, the United States Circuit Court met. The presiding judge was Judge Underwood and Davis was represented by Charles O'Conor. Jefferson Davis appeared leaning on the arm of General Burton, who was his jailor and both walked slowly. It seemed for some reason the government was not ready to proceed and Judge Underwood decided that the prisoner might be admitted to bail. The bail was set at $100,000, the same amount that had been offered as reward for his capture. Gray-haired Horace Greeley of New York, who had branded all Confederates as rebels, volunteered to sign the bail bond and his name headed all the sureties. This was the finest act in Greeley's entire career. The prisoner was discharged.

That night Jefferson Davis and his wife sailed for New York and soon continued on to Canada to join their children, who had never been advised where their father had spent these two years.

After a period of rest during which his eyesight improved, Mr. Davis with the aid of his wife wrote *The Rise and Fall of the Confederacy* and lived to the ripe old age of eighty-one years.

Nearly a century later in 1958, Patrick O'Donovan, Washington correspondent of the London *Observer*, wrote an article in the *New Republic* which proclaimed in its heading that he found Richmond to be "the Saddest Place in America." He wrote:

The image of lighthearted courage, of a city which has been set apart by tragedy will remain. Indeed you could believe that Richmond had never recovered from its destruction and blood-letting at all. It has a withdrawn and muted air. There is a re-fined self discipline and even in the brash and casual shopping streets, a sort of virtue. . . . There are soft and rotten places in among the quiet and unobtrusive streets which vie with Naples. No need to ask who live there. . . . Its sadness has a sweetness about it. But unless *you are of it*, it is not for you.

Of the White House of the Confederacy, he says ". . . it is humble and unforgettable . . . where Jefferson Davis watched the sand run out of the Confederate glass." Many of us who live here "are of it" and live with it with a sort of ease.

XV : THAD STEVENS AND BEN WADE

BACK IN 1792 there had been born in a home of direst poverty, a baby boy with a club foot. Poverty and his malformation had embittered this child, and his mother had labored night and day to earn money to send him to school and later to Dartmouth College. Doubtless some of his associates there had not always been kind and the man while still young had become embit-tered, perhaps not without cause. By 1815, he had been gradu-ated from college and had left Vermont, journeying to Pennsyl-vania where he succeeded in obtaining a position teaching school.

Here also he met with discouragement and although he qualified for admission to the bar, he was at first denied admis-sion on the objection that he was engaged in another occupation while thus qualifying himself. After several attempts, he suc-ceeded in obtaining his license to practice. His admitted single object in life was "to get rich" and he hated and was jealous of the slaveowner. This hatred had been increased by the fact that in 1863 when the Confederates had invaded Pennsylvania, they had burned his iron works near Chambersburg in that state.

He had been elected to the Pennsylvania Legislature in 1833 on the Anti-Masonic ticket and in 1848 was elected to Congress. He was out of Congress for six years but was returned there from the Lancaster District in 1859 and became the Chairman of the powerful Ways and Means Committee in the House of Representatives. He had unusual gifts and he drove men. He was ruthless, but persuasive.

He professed affection for the Negro race and perhaps not without some truth. He never married and if one should desire to journey to Lancaster today, and discreetly inquire, it is possible to be shown a portrait of "Miss Smith," Thad Stevens' Negro mistress or housekeeper, which was the term employed by Mr. Stevens. It is an undisputed fact that this man was buried, by his own request, in a Negro cemetery in Lancaster and Miss Smith was at his deathbed.

Jonathan Blanchard in a letter, once frankly described him thusly: "In every part of the United States people believe that your personal life has been one prolonged sin; that your lips have been defiled with blasphemy; your body with women." Stevens was tall and cadaverous in appearance with a long pale face with gleaming insolent eyes under shaggy brows and a mouth of unusual cruelty; but there was a fascination about his face, similar to the fascination of a snake, as his underlip protruded with the corners depressed. His deformed foot made him bend and limp. He wore an ample brown wig in his late days which included the 'sixties.

While still a young man he had been a continuous drinker and all of his life he continued to be a gambler. Washington was a gambling paradise then, as well as thickly populated with houses of ill fame. The latter were richly furnished and the inmates were mostly young and beautiful and, in many instances, accomplished. In such establishments Thad Stevens as a young man found his pleasures. Perhaps he reasoned, "Why not?" The floors were covered with rich carpeting and from the ceilings hung shining chandeliers with multitudes of gas jets and cut glass globes. One's every want was fulfilled by uniformed Negro attendants in gorgeous livery. Here Thad Stevens could forget his club foot and no one could question his appearance nor his financial status and to him, nothing else mattered.

In the gambling establishments faro was the principal game. In the better of these gambling parlors the games were always "square." Money was not seen on the table, but instead ivory counters were used. Food and wine were free to all who engaged in the games of chance, so it was not unlike a social affair. The proprietor was courtly in manners and often lofty in his bearing. Here Thad Stevens was accepted for what he was, a free spender.

When Congress closed at the end of the day, Stevens would wander down the Avenue from one gambling house to another until hours later he would wander home. A certain story of his gambling instinct is told. It seemed that a committee from a Lancaster church which was undertaking some new building project had come to Washington to solicit a contribution. Stevens was located by them just as he came out of one of his favorite gambling haunts. He had just made a gambling killing and had unsteadily put a dollar bill in one pocket and a hundred dollar bill in the other pocket. After hearing the request inadvertently he reached into the wrong pocket and pulled out the hundred dollar bill and handed it to the soliciting committee. At once realizing his error, he remarked sardonically, "God moves in mysterious ways his wonders to perform," and continued on down the street.

Lincoln disliked this man and this dislike was returned in kind. Stevens' theory of the status of the Southern states could be expressed thusly: These states had seceded and therefore were no longer in the Union; they were no longer American States. They were foreign provinces occupied by Federal troops and as such the United States could deal with them as they saw fit. Slaves could be freed and property confiscated. He was cynically frank and never scrupled as to means toward an end.

Ben Wade of Ohio, known as "Bluff Ben" had served in the Senate for a dozen years. In appearance his head was almost savage, with shaggy eyebrows and beetled brow. He had been anxious for a place on the ticket with Lincoln in 1864 and had not been able to gain the nomination for the vice presidency. He did not approve of Charles Sumner.

Doubtless Senator Sumner from Massachusetts was brilliant, most certainly in his own opinion for he embellished his speeches with quotations in the four languages that he spoke. However this opinion was not shared by Grant and Ben Wade. Grant was not known for his wit but on at least one occasion Wade enjoyed a flash of wit from Grant in regard to Sumner. A reference was made to the fact that some claimed that Sumner did not believe in the Bible, to which Grant countered, "Why should he? He did not write it."

Anyway in March 1867, the Radical Senators named Ben Wade as president pro tem of the Senate and as such he stood in line for the presidency, if by chance Andrew Johnson should be removed.

It was the plan of Thad Stevens to prevent the admission to House and Senate of any newly elected Senators and Representatives from the Southern States. The Constitution declares specifically that "each House shall be the judge of the elections, returns, and qualifications of its members" and if this direction was explicitly followed as Stevens directed, the House could refuse seats to the Southerners, but the Senate, without the lash of such a leader, might not do so.

Stevens' first step was a caucus of all House members that he knew could be depended upon as positive Radicals, with the avowed aim of thwarting the President. He was named by this caucus to prepare the resolutions to pledge both the Senate and House not to admit members from Southern States until the House had agreed. Then a meeting of the whole Republican Party was held to decide what to do with the new members from the so-called Johnson States, meaning those reorganized by the President with Provisional Governments. Stevens had his resolutions in his pocket and his plan for a joint resolution was adopted without a dissenting vote.

This latter meeting was not strictly a Radical meeting, but was attended by many Moderates, and notably by Senators

Sumner and Wade. The moderate Henry J. Raymond, who had been the hero of the Baltimore Convention, was there but on this occasion his spats, monocle and goldheaded cane could not combat the careful plan of venomous Thad Stevens.

Henry Watterson, who had been sent to observe in North Carolina, wrote that there were no more loyal people in Boston than in New Bern, North Carolina where even Negro troops had been stationed. He described the status of secession in North Carolina as comparable to that of the pig in this couplet:

> When it lived, it lived in clover,
> And when it died, it died all over.

But Thad Stevens had no idea of letting punishment and persecution die. When the Clerk of the House of Representatives called the roll of the House on December 4, he did as he had been instructed, he had omitted the names of every single man of a Southern State. Horace Maynard, Congressman-at-Large from Tennessee rose to his feet and demanded that his name be called, but the Clerk remained silent.

James Brooks of New York, the Democratic leader, rose to demand, "If Tennessee is not in the Union and has not been in the Union, and is not a loyal state, and the people of Tennessee are aliens and foreigners to the Union, by what right does the President of the United States usurp a place in the White House?" No answer. Brooks continued, "I wish to know when the matter of admitting Southern members will be taken up."

To this Stevens curtly replied, "I will press the matter at the proper time." When he sat down, for some reason his heavy brown wig had become slightly awry, but he still smiled sardonically in blissful ignorance of his appearance.

Sumner offered a resolution much like that made by Stevens, when the Senate convened, and except that the Senate required a joint vote for admission of the new Senators, the requirements were not changed.

Andrew Johnson's plan to return the Southern States to representation in both houses of Congress had failed. Thad Stevens' plan of intrigue had won the day.

XVI : THE BLACK CODES OF THE SOUTH

THE PROBLEM OF THE NEGRO did not start in 1861. It had perplexed America since 1620 and still perplexes it today. Perhaps it always will.

Charles Sumner had a large circle of acquaintances. Not the least distinguished of these was the scientist, Louis Agassiz. In 1863, Agassiz had written:

> We should beware how we give to the blacks rights, by virtue of which they may endanger the progress of the whites before their temper has been tested by prolonged experience. Social equality I deem at all times impractical, a natural impossibility from the very character of the Negro race. . . . No man has a right to what he is unfit to use. Our best rights have been acquired successively. I cannot, therefore, think it just or safe to grant at once all the privileges which we ourselves have acquired by long struggles. History teaches us what terrible reactions have followed too rapid and too extensive changes. Let us beware of granting too much to the Negro race in the beginning lest it become necessary hereafter to deprive them of some of the privileges which they may use to their and our own detriment.

Lincoln once told a committee of Negroes to whom he talked during 1862, your race suffers from living among us, ours from your presence."

Negro suffrage was not an issue for which the war was fought. The states from which the Radicals came did not grant suffrage to the Negro, yet Negro suffrage became the lying slogan of these so-called patriots.

And so the "black codes" were evolved in the wake of Appomattox. The first was adopted by the Mississippi Legislature in October of 1865. Under the Mississippi apprentice law all Negroes under eighteen years of age must be apprenticed by the probate court to some white person, the Negro's former owner to have the preference in securing the right of his services. The master must make bond to the state to furnish his apprentice with clothing and food, to treat him without cruelty, care for him medically and to teach him to read and write. The master was to be given the power of chastisement as a father would be allowed to inflict on his child. If the apprentice should run away, he could be recaptured and jailed. If any other man enticed the apprentice away, the man so offending against the apprenticeship law could be found guilty of high misdemeanor.

The vagrancy law of the same state was even more stringent. All Negroes found without employment on the second Monday of January 1866 and unlawfully assembling and white persons assembling with Negroes, would be deemed vagrants and therefore fined and sent to jail. If the Negro was unable to pay his fine, the sheriff should hire him out to any man who would for the shortest period of time of service pay the fine and court costs. Again the preference was given to the former employer of the Negro, who usually was the former master. Also a poll tax of one dollar a year was levied on each Negro, and if he failed to pay this, he was adjudged a vagrant and subject to fine, sentence and hiring out.

However under a Civil Rights Act, Negroes might acquire property, sue or be sued but no Negro could rent or lease any lands or house except in the incorporated cities or towns. Unless he had a lawful home and an officer's certificate to prove it, he was liable to arrest. If he quit his job before his contract expired, he forfeited all wages, or he could be arrested and returned to his employer. No Negro could keep firearms or bowie knives. For many years he was not allowed to ride in a first class passenger car, unless traveling with mistresses as maids.

Naturally the Radicals thought it outrageous that an act which was not an offense when committed by a white man, became a misdemeanor or felony, when committed by a member of the black race. These laws were undoubtedly aimed at the Negro race. Possibly they were instigated from the problem of fear of the actions of the Negro in a society largely rural and in communities in which the Negro population greatly outnumbered the white as was true in Mississippi.

Alabama's black code differed somewhat from that of her sister state. Here a vagrant was defined as any stubborn or refractory servant and also servants who loitered away their time. Any such servant thus accused might be brought before a justice of the peace and fined fifty dollars. If he was unable to pay the fine, he was to be hired out for six months. The Radicals claimed that the idea of this six months limitation was to fine Negroes for a half year and secure their services for the period of crop making, especially the hoeing and harvesting of cotton and then to be relieved of supporting the Negro during the winter and idle months of farming. In this code the language did not limit execution of the law to Negroes, but doubtless was limited to the Negro race in actual execution. According to Blaine:

> There may have been more cruel laws enacted, but the statute books of the world might be searched in vain for one meaner in intent.

In South Carolina the codes provided for enforced apprenticeship, with the master having the right to inflict moderate chastisement which was not otherwise defined. Contracts for service from servant to master defined what proper service a farm hand to a master constituted. This code was passed by the South Carolina Legislature in December 1865. Doubtless these farming communities were attempting to ready themselves for the spring farming for 1866. The hours of labor were defined from sunrise to sunset and stipulated that servants should rise at dawn, do various chores of feeding, watering and caring for stock, prepare the meals and begin the regular farm work by sunrise. Servants were accountable for all property in their care; damaged, lost or stolen. A servant must not leave the farm premises without the consent of the master, and if he quit, he forfeited all wages due him. However, he might legally quit, if he did not receive wholesome food or if he were the victim of unauthorized battery on his person. The code also stated that no Negro could pursue a craft or trade such as artisan, mechanic or shopkeeper without first obtaining a license from the judge of the district court, which license was good for one year only. The only employment which was not so licensed was that of husbandry. The Negro must pay a license of $10 to pursue the simplest craft, although no such licenses were required of white men. The rate of such license was set at $100 per year for a merchant or peddler, which was an impossible sum for a Negro to secure.

The Negroes thought that the government was surely going to give each and every male Negro "forty acres and a mule." As a matter of fact, Thaddeus Stevens in a speech at Lancaster, Pennsylvania, on September 6 of that year did disclose a homestead plan by which 70,000 Rebels who owned 200 acres each were to have their lands confiscated and divided among the Negroes. Just how this land was to be apportioned among the Negro race was not elaborated upon in this speech.

A group of Northern sharpers did a thriving business by selling four little blue pointed pegs to the gullible Negroes, telling them that they could drive these little pegs on any forty acres of their former master's land and the land thus pegged would be theirs legally. Negroes flocked to cities by thousands and vagrancy laws of some type were sorely needed.

Plantation owners found it impossible to secure farm workers and there were cases of suicide among planters who, in some instances, gave up in despondency. Strychnine could be bought at country stores and there were cases in which despondent planters took the poison rather than use it to poison the destructive crows for which it was intended.

To embarrass the President, Stevens, Sumner, and Wade summoned to Washington, Frederick Douglass, a Negro orator and agitator and a group of Negro leaders, whom they coached in detail as to what to say to Mr. Johnson. When they appeared Johnson shook hands kindly with each of the Negroes. Douglass then informed him that they were not satisfied with the amendment prohibiting slavery, but that they wished it to be enforced by appropriate legislation. Apparently Mr. Johnson did not realize that the purpose of the interview was to embarrass him. He told the delegation that he was a friend of the colored man but that he did not wish to see one race try to exterminate the other; and that the states were the depositories of their own political power governing suffrage. He ended by saying that he did not pretend to be wiser than Providence or stronger than the laws of nature. Douglass attempted to argue loudly with the President, expostulating so vehemently that the President was forced to tell the Negro that he would not enter into a controversy. Douglass countered by saying that the President was sending the delegation to the people and they would go to the people.

On the next day the delegation wrote an open letter to the President stating that his views were "entirely unsound." The following night Frederick Douglass made a grossly abusive and insulting speech in Philadelphia regarding the President.

In contrast to this happening, shortly thereafter a certain Episcopal minister from Columbia, South Carolina called on Mr. Johnson and advised him of a plan by the church to found a school for Negro children in Charleston. Mr. Johnson was enthusiastic about the plan and offered the aid of the administration, and moreover added that he would send a personal check for one thousand dollars, which he promptly did.

A Freedmen's Bureau had been established as an agency of the War Department in March 1865 to aid helpless, ignorant Negroes until they could provide for and take care of themselves. Now a Freedmen's Bureau Bill passed the Senate and the House. It guaranteed civil rights to all Negroes and if any Negro were not accorded thorough equality, an agent of the Freedmen's Bureau could act as a court to impose a fine or imprisonment on any person who deprived the Negro of this right. On February 22, 1866, Johnson vetoed this bill.

Many historians claim that this Washington's Birthday Speech, in which Andrew Johnson vetoed the Freedmen's Bill, was the beginning of his downfall. But the veto was applauded by many. He was hailed as comparable with Andrew Jackson, Old Hickory. His enemies claimed that he was drunk when he made the speech, his friends praised him and some pressed him to reorganize his Cabinet.

During this period the President's mail was filled with personal appeals for help. A widow, who said that he had before this furnished her transportation out of his own pocket, asked for further help. An old journeyman tailor, who had once worked for Mr. Johnson, sought his help with evident confidence that it would be granted; part of both feet had been carried off by a shell, and he wanted ten of fifteen dollars to take him back to his friends.

There was no organized government assistance for these cases and the records show that the President could and did answer these simple pleas personally. In his administration, for the first time, records were kept at the White House. Now in the Manuscript Division of the Congressional Library at Washington, it is possible to see receipts for hats and shoes and pink leaflets containing the Sunday School lessons of his small grandchildren, side by side with the gravest political documents.

In one record book there is an amusing entry detailing the plea of an Episcopal minister, who evidently was disapproving, and who desired to be released from his obligation to pray for the President of the United States.

XVII : WASHINGTON HOTELS AND HABITS IN 1865

JUST BEYOND THE TREASURY BUILDING at the next corner stood the White House, sometimes called informally "the President's House." The bull frogs often croaked and it was something of a kine pasture, according to one description. Ague and fever were prevalent in the Spring and Autumn and for this reason the White House was considered neither healthful nor desirable as a residence. The main structure had been designed on the lines of the palace of the Duke of Leinster and was surrounded by handsome grounds, which in the rear consisted of a park which extended to the banks of the Potomac. The house had been partially burned in 1814 by Admiral Cockburn's raiders, but had been rebuilt. It was built of freestone, painted white, hence the name. One legend insists that it was named for the Widow Custis' home on the peninsula, which home was burned during the War of Secession while it was the residence of a son of Robert E. Lee and his son's wife, Charlotte Lee.

The White House is two stories high and is surrounded by a balustrade. On the north front there is a portico with four Ionic columns. The main entrance leads from this front portico through a doorway into the main hall. The house had thirty-one rooms, all of large size according to the custom of the day. From the wall of the main hall, which is divided in the center by imitation marble pillars, there hung the portraits of the first sixteen presidents. On the left, and occupying the whole eastern side of the house was the East Room, which was lavishly furnished, much of it having been done by Mrs. Lincoln. In this room all formal receptions were held, and also all state dinners. There were four massive fireplaces, but the heat thus furnished was not sufficient to heat so large an apartment, and guests often shivered as they ate. The Blue Room, Red Room and Green Room adjoined the East Room and were furnished in the colors for which they were named. Immediately west of the Red Room was the large dining room which could be used for smaller state dinners. Next to this large dining room, was the smaller dining room, which was intended to be used by the President and his family.

On the second floor, on the north side, there were six bedrooms used by the President and his family, and on the south side were seven rooms—antechamber, audience room, the President's private office, the Cabinet Room, the ladies' parlor and two other rooms, which could be used for any designated purpose.

In the basement were eleven rooms used for kitchens, pantries, butlers' rooms, maids' rooms, etc. The stairway was to the left of the main entrance. On this stairway, a doorkeeper was always stationed to prevent unauthorized persons from entering but no other precautions were taken at this era for protection or privacy. The house was furnished with the idea of costliness but, except for lavishness and elegance, there was no especial taste or comfort visible.

When Mr. Lincoln occupied the White House, he was accessible to visitors at almost any waking hour, except that he would see no one before nine o'clock in the morning. Andrew Johnson was, if anything, more accessible to visitors than Mr. Lincoln. Eliza Johnson never made any known comments to discourage this, as did Mary Todd Lincoln, and perhaps Mrs. Lincoln was right. Edward McManus, a shrewd little Irishman with a pleasant smile, was at the door in the Lincoln Administration and for several presidents before and also for Mr. Johnson. Mr. McManus could usually tell what a visitor wanted and during the Lincoln Administration, they usually were office seekers. The remainder of the Presidential day was consumed with Cabinet meetings, reading the Washington newspapers and discussions with office holders.

Beginning in 1861 President Lincoln and his family had lived, during the summer, at Soldiers' Home about three miles north of Washington. However by 8:30 every morning Mr. Lincoln would call for his carriage and he would be on his way to his Presidential office. As the Johnson family was not able to move into the White House until summer, they did not go to Soldiers' Home in the summer of 1865.

The White House was not occupied by Andrew Johnson until after June 9, 1865, since it was not until this date that Mary Todd Lincoln found it convenient to move. Shortly after, the Johnson family moved to Washington from Greeneville, Tennessee. Eliza Johnson, now invalided from consumption, had her bedroom on the northeast front on the second floor overlooking the lawn, and just opposite the library in which her husband spent much time. The other five bedrooms were taxed to capacity to provide space for the twelve members of the Johnson family and the two extra rooms were pressed into use for bedrooms. The President's two married daughters, Mrs. Patterson and Mrs. Stover, now a widow, and their famiiles were in the White House with their parents. There were five grandchildren and two unmarried sons, Robert and Andrew Jr.

In this vicinity were located the most famous of Washington's hotels. The National was the largest in the city and was located at the corner of Sixth Street and Pennsylvania Avenue. This hotel was the Washington home of John Wilkes Booth, and had been the favorite stopping place of the Southern aristocracy before the War. It was during the administration of James Buchanan that this famous hostelry had the doubtful distinction of having a disease named for it. It was the "National Hotel Disease," resulting from the lack of kitchen sanitation and it doubtless flourished in other kitchens than those of the National. Its well known proprietor was John Gadsby and it was often spoken of simply as "Gadsby's."

Sometime in the 'forties a rival establishment was opened on the opposite corner, at first known as the Indian Queen, later as Brown's Hotel, from the name of the proprietor, Jesse Brown, and still later in the Civil War becoming known as the famous Metropolitan.

Going up the Avenue, at the corner of Twelfth Street was the much less pretentious Kirkwood House in which Andrew Johnson was living when he took the oath of office as the seventeenth President of the United States on April 15, 1865. It was a bountiful inn and well suited to the requirements of an unpretentious man, such as the Vice-President.

Caleb Willard was undoubtedly the most enterprising hotel keeper that early Washington had ever known. Two blocks west he had built the rambling structure that bore his name, six stories high and more than a hundred yards square. Unpretentious guests could take a room on the top floor and get excellent exercise by climbing five flights of stairs, better for the leg muscles than the back. It may have been truthfully said that "more scheming, plotting, planning heads, more aching and joyful hearts, than any building of the same size in the world" were housed in the Willard during the War. It was certainly packed to capacity with politicians during these bloody years. It was thus described by W. H. Russell, correspondent of the London *Times*. He was startled with the rapidity with which doors kept opening and shutting for men with papers bulging out of their pockets. The hostelry was full of people seeking interviews with Senators and Congressmen and finding them, then presenting them with documents of recommendations for federal jobs. Little of this ceased under the Johnson Administration and during 1866 the rabble increased. A war boom was born, the likes of which had never been seen in Washington before.

Some 2,500 persons dined in the Willard's dining rooms, which has been described as "a vast apartment without carpets or any furniture but plain chairs and tables, ranged in close rows." The English correspondent, Mr. Russell, noted that a typical breakfast menu consisted of black tea and toast, fresh spring shad, scrambled eggs, pig's feet fried in batter, wild pigeons, two robins on toast, Thomas' bread, waffles and syrup, and hot biscuit. There was a handsome drawing room, with pianos, sofas and easy chairs for the ladies. For convenience there was a barber shop complete with publicity and parley.

It seemed that the bulk of the population lived in hotels. Editorial comment in the New York *Independent* complained on January 22, 1868 that too many people in the Federal Babylon lived in hotels. The editorial continued by saying, "If the Government were to provide for every Senator and Representative a comfortable house to live in, surrounded by his family . . . public morals would be visibly improved and private manners visibly refined." And one is inclined to agree with Theodore Tilton, the editor of the *Independent*.

The hotel trade was loudly solicited at the railroad station by the loud shouts of omnibus and hack drivers, known as Jehus, a Biblican term from Jehu, the son of Nimshi, who drove his chariot furiously. Along New Jersey Avenue, at the time of the arrival of trains, one was treated to a battle of words that would unnerve all except the most stolid.

"Metropolitan Hotel, sir. Only first class house in the city," or "This way for the National. Best house in the whole city," announced the followers of John Gadsby. But loudest of all were the announcers for the Willard, "Willard, everybody's going to the Willard. Every gemmen knows Willard's. This way, sur." Wartime in Washington did not lack zest or vigor of the lungs.

The station itself was a frame building with a tower and clock, which stood at the corner of New Jersey Avenue and C Street. It was dirty and cheerless but adequate for the times. The steam locomotive had only been used since 1830 and now, less than four decades later, the trip from Baltimore to Washington, a distance of forty miles, was made eight times daily. The slowest trains consumed one hour and fifty minutes to cover the forty miles and some fast schedules consumed only one hour and twenty minutes. Some passenger cars closely resembled a large cart on wheels, while others were not too dissimilar from the coach-type passenger cars of today. All trains were controlled by hand brakes, had open platforms, and were heated by large cast iron stoves, often heated red hot. The trainmen were truly uniformed in splendor in double-breasted light blue uniforms, with ornate brass buttons, and military caps bearing the employee's title on a metal plate on the front. Also there was one other scheduled frequenter of all trains who did a bustling business by carrying trays of gum drops, lemon drops, tobacco, apples, and cakes for sale. From this old station Lincoln entered for his first inauguration and from it the body of the murdered president was carried to its burial place in Springfield. This station was used until 1905.

These were the days when Engine Builder Thatcher Perkins built his famous locomotive the "Ten Wheel Perkins." The engines were all wood burners, and occasionally it was necessary for the train to stop for replenishment of its fuel supply along the way, at stations stocked for this need. Thus the Washington Branch of the B. & O. was operated after stopping at the Relay House, nine miles southwest of Baltimore. The railroad fare for this journey was $1.60, a small amount indeed in comparison with the amounts necessarily charged by the stage coach lines formerly. It was getting to be a fast age.

Any traveler from the South had to arrive by boat on the Potomac, unless he came afoot or on horseback or on one of the very few stage lines. The country roads, as well as the streets of Washington had almost unfathomless mud, and along the railroad line between Washington and Baltimore, the stations were nothing more than hamlets. The farmhouses were dingy and far between and were whitewashed rather than painted. The fields were full of stagnant pools with pigs, geese, and children making full use of them at the same time. During the War, the scene was enlivened with soldiers, military warehouses, and camps.

Entering the City of Washington, the Capitol Building at once burst into view. Major L'Enfant, the Frenchman, who had drawn up the plan of the city, had planned the Capitol as the starting point and center of the city. George Washington had selected the western brow of a commanding hill to give a view of the surrounding country. It had been completed when James Monroe had been President and in 1850, an extension had been made to the original building.

It was built of pure white marble, with a magnificent dome, constructed entirely of iron held together with a maze of bars and bolts. Halfway up the dome was a gallery running around the exterior of the dome's outer shell. This could be reached by an iron stairway, and still higher was a gallery just beneath the canopy nearly 200 feet above the floor below.

There was a heating and ventilating apparatus, accompanied by hissing steam and noisy apparatus, but the superintendent probably was justly proud of the clanging machinery, efficient for the times. Also there were "members" baths finished in black walnut with shower baths as well as tubs and the floor was laid with marble tiles.

The Capitol restaurant was managed by a Negro with possibly the most elegant manners to be observed in the Capitol. His bill of fare included anything that could be had at the season and was served in perfect style of the day.

Pennsylvania Avenue had once been paved from the Capitol to Georgetown, but in less than six months after the War began, it became so worn and grooved by army wagons that in many places more than ten inches of mud covered the pavements and army wagons and mules became stalled. In dry weather this mud changed by usage into clouds of dust. The sidewalks along the Avenue were of brick but their condition was deplorable due to deposits of mud and dust from the streets. By the time of Lincoln's second inauguration the streets were covered with a thick coat of mud. Washington residents feared to bring their private carriages out for fear of miring them in the rut tracks. In spite of all this Pennsylvania Avenue was alive with life and motion.

Business was on the boom. Vendors were on the corners, hawking their wares of soaps that would remove any grease spot and Italians roasted chestnuts dipped in butter to put the spots obligingly back on again. A peddler sold artificial insects, which jumped up and down from a string, and men offered their telescopes at ten cents a look. To this was added owners of lung testing machines, who declared that they could tell you just what kind of chest you had in these days of consumption, but they often did not take precedence over the organ grinders and dancing monkeys.

Nor was traffic unregulated. On every street corner mounted guards sat with drawn swords to pounce upon whoever could in some mysterious way be guilty of speeding, true ancestors of their present day counterparts. A two or three minute schedule was maintained by the horse drawn cars over the double track from the Navy Yard to Georgetown.

The shops were a motley assortment. In the same block, could be found shops that sold satin by the yard, hay by the bale or coffins to the individual, even advertising and suggesting embalming with a covering of a transparency. One could be wrapped in satin or paraffin, as one desired. The north side of the street was the better side for on the former side often there were painted index fingers pointing out the whereabouts of a washwoman or a cook. Buildings were taller on the north side and housed the better shops.

However, withal, Washington was a shabby city. During the War a traveller from a European city, expressed his opinions that there was "no State in the world which possesses proportionately so small, scantily populated and shabby a capital as the American Union." At this time there were few statues and monuments, no modern school buildings of any kind, and few theaters, the best known being Ford's and Grover's. North and east of the Capitol the city had few houses and after one passed Fourteenth Street, they were especially scattered until Georgetown was reached. The only government buildings of any great size were the White House; the Capitol; the Treasury Building, in which Andrew Johnson first had his office after Lincoln's murder; and the Interior Building. At one end of the Treasury Building there was attached an old ramshackled brick building in which the Secretary of State had his office, when Seward was Secretary. The War Building was originally a two-storied building made of brick, painted a dull shade, and equipped with a frame porch with clumsy columns. Late in the war period a third story was added with no semblance of plan nor symmetry. The Washington Monument had been begun before the War but was left unfinished, with two-thirds of it uncompleted. In a careless, neglected manner the ugly sheds, stones, and scraps of unused lumber had been left at the base of the uncompleted monument. Late in 1863 the Post Office Building and the Patent Office Building were completed.

An unpleasant odor arose from the B Street Canal and slow Tiber Creek, as well as from other open pools, ditches and swamps making a mosquito's life an unending holiday. There was no attempt at control of animals and pigs, goats, cows, and horses roamed at will and grazed where they liked.

At the inauguration of 1861, a new type of citizen had appeared to the consternation of the people of Washington. They came from the West, doubtless due partly to their admiration for this man Lincoln, but bringing with them the ideas and habits of the Western gamblers, speculators, and, often with them came females of easy virtue. The lady "whose name was Lou" was now plying her trade in Washington. The men came to make the largest possible profit out of the goods they sold to the government or to individuals and were interested in profit and not patriotism.

Here was a paradise for gamblers. In 1863 an official report listed no less than 163 admitted gambling establishments, many of which were sumptuously furnished. Most of them were situated on or near Pennsylvania Avenue and had heavily curtained windows and an air of mysterious silence. Probably Thad Stevens was the most constant frequenter of these, but he was joined by other Senators and Congressmen and the so-called better class. Tables were piled with every conceivable delicacy and banquets were served without charge to the gambling patrons. Although Congress had passed a law prohibiting the sale of liquor to soldiers under penalty of fine or imprisonment, little heed was paid to this unenforceable law, and the same aforementioned report listed 3700 fountains featuring beer barrels and whiskey demijohns. Saloons were closed by order of the mayor from midnight to 9 A.M. but the hotels and restaurants could stay open, and who cared where he drank, just so that his thirst was abated. In the worst of these places the only equipment was a gallon of liquor and a rusty tin cup, with whiskey dispensed at ten cents a drink. One trick of the trade was to dispense liquor from a wooden cask and when the cask was emptied, it was refilled with water and with some flavor remaining, the second filling was sold at the same price as the first to the half-drunks.

A type of entertainment known as the Canterburies arose. These were a kind of concert ball with indecent brutal performances, at which victims were often drugged, murdered or rolled for the amount of money in their pockets. The victims of the latter practice were all too often soldiers on leave with their pay in their pockets.

Next on the agenda of entertainment were Washington's

more or less fashionable houses of ill fame. The residents were usually young, beautiful, and not natives of Washington, but they came in from New York, Boston or Chicago and stayed for the full session of Congress. They were representative but not apportioned according to population. Such houses were furnished lavishly and operated in grandiose style. They were frequented by those who could pay and doctors, lawyers, Governors and members of Congress spoke to each other openly as though they were guests in the homes of mutual friends.

In this medley of a city the social standards were unpredictable. Men engaged in trade were definitely looked down upon by politicians and others. Money was the only standard by which one journeyed from one social class to a higher one. One Washingtonian who had just inherited a fortune, as soon as feasible made this remark, "I never did a day's work in my life and never will." No woman of the better social class would admit to having soiled her hands with working. Into this bedlam, there moved the family of Andrew Johnson in 1865, with the background of Eliza McArdle and her mother having made their living by sewing cloth sandals and Polly Doherty, mother of the President, having done the laundry of the members of the North Carolina Supreme Court.

During this time, householders charged fabulous rents and others hastily built shabby shacks for which even higher rents were exacted. Washington had been a small city of some 60,000 residents and had now swelled to a quarter of a million residents and remained at this peak level throughout the War period.

At least twenty-one hospitals were scattered throughout the city caring for more than 14,000 wounded, mangled, and smoke-blackened soldiers. At one time the huge convalescent camp at Alexandria attempted to care for 10,000, being so overcrowded that some of the men had to sleep on the ground in midwinter. Undisciplined soldiers roamed the streets day and night, a situation with which the local police were inadequate to cope.

The game of faro was the favorite game of the gambling casinos. It was reliably reported that nine of ten of the shortages of government paymasters could be traced to losses at the faro banks, where money was exchanged for ivory counters. Female faro dealers were used to lure the unwary from the Capitol or his hotel. First the victim was made drunk, then forced to play and swindled out of his bank roll. This was Washington's heyday.

XVIII : ANDREW AND ELIZA'S PERSONAL TROUBLES

INTO THE WHITE HOUSE in 1865 there moved a couple past middle age, sincerely devoted to each other. Neither Andrew Johnson nor his wife was in robust health; Eliza was practically an invalid, but her consumption was not of the so-called "galloping" kind, but rather a slowly progressive type and she was to live throughout her husband's occupancy of the White House, both to her surprise and that of her family. The accepted treatment for her disease was to stay indoors and to burn lightwood pine knots of wood and inhale the fumes of the turpentine from the burning wood. She outlived her husband some six months.

Andrew Johnson had long had a kidney ailment which at times, when he had attacks of kidney stones, caused him excruciating pain. At that time hypodermics were not known as a treatment.

These parents had lost one son, Dr. Charles Johnson, during the War. His death was not directly due to the conflict; he had been killed as the result of a fall from a horse during the siege of Nashville. Their second son, Robert, remained and the youngest child of all, Andrew, Jr. was then only thirteen.

As long as possible Mr. Johnson kept the information from his wife that their son, Colonel Robert Johnson, who was serving as one of his father's secretaries, was a hopeless inebriate. The father consulted physicians about his son's weakness and they advised him that there might be some hope of reclaiming the young man, if he could be kept from alcohol for a prolonged period of time. This could scarcely be done in the atmosphere of Washington.

It was at this time that Mr. Johnson talked the matter over with his wife. Gideon Welles had been Lincoln's Secretary of the Navy and he still occupied this position in the Johnson Cabinet. He had been born in Connecticut and had been editor of the Hartford *Times* for eleven years. He was a handsome man and he had done an excellent job of handling the blockade during the War with the Confederacy. He was a friend of the President and now Mr. Johnson went to him anxiously with the hope of rehabilitating his son, Robert. It seemed that Mr. Welles doubted whether Robert could be rehabilitated but when the plan was explained to him, he realized that the President should be relieved of the care and anxiety of dealing with Robert's excesses and so agreed to help with the plan.

Mr. Welles was to arrange for a sea voyage for the President's son on the U.S.S. *Chattanooga,* then ready to set sail for Liberia. This exact trip was the idea of Mr. Welles, but when it was suggested to the President he was in hearty accord. However, Mr. Johnson felt that Robert should have some reason or duties for going on such a trip. Therefore Welles consulted with Mr. Seward, then Secretary of State, and it was decided to commission Colonel Robert Johnson to look into the slave trade for, after all, he was capable and as attractive as his father, if only he could be kept sober. The paymaster of the *Chattanooga* was given a check from the Department of State for Robert's expenses but with the express instructions that not any part of this amount was to be spent except under the express instructions of the Commander of the *Chattanooga.*

Thus a sad problem was disposed of, at least temporarily. Gideon Welles had proved himself to be the "perfect brick" as the President had previously described him. There were other things even more pressing on the President than the inebrity of probably his best beloved son.

Perhaps this partial solution of a problem of long standing had a healthful effect on Eliza Johnson for it was about this time that she received, for the first time, at the White House. John Hay had just retired as Secretary of the United States legation in Paris and had come to Washington for a brief visit. There was a reception at the White House, to which Mr. Hay was invited and he recalled Mrs. Johnson as receiving for the first time. He said that she was quiet; one could scarcely expect her to be vivacious. He said that the group was not as good as average; not distinguished, but not squalid and added that they used to have plenty of both. He also recalled that the White House was much more richly furnished than in his time. Most of this had been done by Mrs. Lincoln.

The President was cordial to Mr. Hay and on another occasion he was taken to the White House to make his bow to Mrs. Patterson and to Mrs. Stover.

XIX : WHAT THE HISTORIES DO NOT TELL

NEARLY TWO YEARS HAD PASSED since Appomattox. The year 1867 had begun. Thad Stevens was exerting all of his power to bring about the degradation of the South. What a pleasurable thing it would be to watch white men, and particularly white women writhe under the domination of the Negro. What a heyday for the carpet baggers. So far as is known no white woman, except his mother, had ever known any affection for this venomous man. Could this be revenge for scorn, either real or imaginary? "For two years ten states have endured all of the horrors of anarchy. . . . Persecution, exile and murder have been the order of the day," he shouted. Under Stevens' Reconstruction measure "the pretended state governments" of Virginia, North and South Carolina, Georgia, Florida, Alabama, Louisiana, Mississippi, Texas and Arkansas were wiped out and this vast territory was to be divided into five military districts, with Virginia set up as Military District No. 1 and the remaining states to be divided into four additional military districts. According to this bill passed by the House and pushed through by the able and despotic leadership of Stevens, the military governors were not to be named by the President, but they were to be picked by the General of the Army—that is, Grant, who by this time had been taken over by the Radicals. These military governors could dismiss governors, suspend elections, annul orders of courts, and rule in absolute despotism.

The Senate could not stomach the bill unamended but did pass it with the amendment by Senator Sherman. This Sherman was the brother of General Sherman. The President, according to the amendment was to appoint the military governors and a method was provided by which the States so affected could finally resume their full national authority. At least one Senator, Saulsbury of Delaware declared, "There is not a single provision in the bill that is constitutional or will stand up in a court of justice."

Garfield with some glow of pride said, "It was written with a steel pen made out of a bayonet." To aid the rule of the carpet-bagger, a provision provided that male citizens of whatever color, with one year's residence, not disqualified by felony or participation in rebellion, could vote. Grant had told Lee that his soldiers would be allowed to return to their homes not to be disturbed by the United States authority so long as they observed their paroles. Now they were disqualified to vote.

On Washington's Birthday, the President presented the Reconstruction Bill for consideration by his Cabinet and not a member approved, except Stanton. Stanton wanted to approve it; all other members advised a veto. Johnson's Washington Birthday Speech is not included in the histories. "Under this bill," Johnson declared, "each commanding officer would become an absolute monarch, with the power to delegate this absolute power to any number of deputies, that he might see fit to appoint. Such power has not been wielded by any monarch in England in five hundred years. No master ever had control so absolute over the slaves as this bill gives to the military officers over both white and colored persons." Johnson fully divined the black decade that was to follow.

Only two days remained to override the President's veto.

It was enough for Thad Stevens. He asked for a suspension of rules, which was done. The House repassed the bill 135 to 48 and the Senate concurred with 38 to 10. The blackest page that ever disgraced the statute books was thus written on March 4, 1867.

It is not to be forgotten that Senator McDougal joined Senator Saulsbury of Delaware in opposition to Stevens' Reconstruction Bill, inquiring how any man could suppose that intelligent, white men would allow themselves to be governed by Negroes "as ignorant as a horse in a stable about all things that belong to government." Doubtless this statement was true for the Negro of that era had had absolutely no opportunity to learn even how to read or write and certainly no training or knowledge of the functions of government.

There was another type of Negro who did not engage in all this political horse play. Some of the ex-slaves stayed on the plantations of their former masters voluntarily. Still others had their fling at freedom and later returned to beg leave to live again in their former cabins and work for wages, necessarily small. They always received rations and residence gratis from employers.

One of these, "Aunt" Martha Shaw was still living on the tobacco plantation of the son of her former owner after the turn of the century. She still cooked in her fireplace on a four legged skillet. She had raised her family of children. One day upon being questioned as to who her husband had been, she naively replied, "Lawsy, child, I ain't never been bothered wid no husband," and then she reminiscently turned her baking sweet potato over in the ashes.

XX : TENURE OF OFFICE BILL

BENJAMIN WADE KNEW that, as President of the Senate, the removal of Andrew Johnson would make him President of the United States. Even his wife was smug about the possibility of becoming the First Lady. Wade was now stealthily in search of worthwhile material.

Lafayette Baker had been chief of the Nation's detective bureau and he had been dismissed by Johnson. Could not Baker furnish something of value? Indeed he could and would. He claimed that back in 1865 a certain man in Nashville had shown him a letter written by Johnson to Jefferson Davis, while Johnson had been military governor of Tennessee. He said that a colored servant of Parson Brownlow's son had stolen the letter from Johnson's desk before it was sent and that this man Adamson would sell it if the offer were sufficient. Naturally the letter was never found nor produced and Baker averred that its contents offered to turn the whole power Johnson possessed in Tennessee over to the rebel cause for certain conditions. It mattered not that no one short of an imbecile would have written out such in long hand, for one lie was as good as another. Furthermore, his broken arm rendered Johnson unable to write easily before this time.

The Tenure of Office Bill provided that civil officers in whose appointment the Senate had participated could not be removed without the advice and consent of the Senate, but there was a further proviso that, "the Secretaries of State, of the Treasury, of War, of the Navy and of the Interior, the Postmaster-General, and the Attorney-General, shall hold their offices respectively for and during the term of the President by whom they have been appointed and for one month thereafter, subject to the removal by and with the advice and consent of the Senate."

Attorney-General Stanbery and Stanton, who had once been Attorney-General, were voluble in their denunciation of the bill and with ostentatious vehemence Mr. Stanton declared "any man who would remain in his seat in the Cabinet when his advice was not wanted was unfit for the place." Johnson vetoed it but on the very day that it reached the House, it was re-passed by a majority of two-thirds in both houses of Congress.

Grave troubles had arisen in the execution of the Reconstruction Bill and it was the hope of the President that the Supreme Court would display the same courage as his veto and declare the bill unconstitutional. Stanton as Secretary of War, had become increasingly Radical in his views within the past months and the President had given the faithless minister to understand that his continuance in the Cabinet was not desired. However Stanton's skin was leathery and impervious to mere hints. The President held a conference with Grant who argued strongly against the removal of Stanton. Both Stanton and Grant had changed within the year and it was commonly reported that Grant's answer was influenced by Stanton.

An incident demonstrating Stanton's duplicity concerned the trial of John Surratt. Surratt had fled to Canada, thence to Britain and still later to Italy. There he had enlisted in the Papal Army but he had finally been arrested and brought back to Washington for trial, almost two years after the execution of his mother.

Some ten days before the trial ended, at which time Sanford Conover, the star witness for the Radicals who had been convicted for perjury and was about to be removed to the Albany Penitentiary, planned one last move. His wife called upon Mr. Johnson and left with him a petition signed by Judge Holt and Riddle and also a letter from Ashley, all Radicals. Mrs. Conover told the President that promises and assurances of pardons had been given her husband by certain parties on the condition that he would do certain things but that they had been put off until the Conovers did not know what to think of it. Inadvertently another note from Ashley had been enclosed with the petition, and this note provoked the President to further inquiry. Now Conover determined to expose the scoundrels with whom he had dealt for surely there was no reason for him to protect them. He sent his wife back to see the President denouncing the Secretary of War and now the farce began between Stanton, incumbent Secretary of War and General Lorenzo Thomas, who had been Adjutant-General, but whose duties during the War had been confined to the examination of soldier cemeteries. General Thomas called on Mr. Stanton, and delivered a note from the President, relieving Stanton of his duties as Secretary of War. To this Stanton replied, "I do not know whether I will obey your instructions or whether I will resist them." General Thomas led the President to believe that Stanton acquiesced in his acceptance of removal. However just the opposite was true. As soon as Thomas had left, Stanton prepared a formal message to Congress notifying it of the President's action in his attempted removal and he sent private notes to many Senators, entreating their aid. He ordered Grant to station a guard about the building and around his office. For several weeks thereafter his office became his permanent residence and he ate and slept there and as it was February, perhaps he did not bathe.

The President's new Secretary of War *ad interim*, which was the status of General Thomas' appointment, did not see Stanton further that day but his hours were not idly spent that day and most assuredly not that night. Sometime in the early evening, the old General talked to an old crony, to a reporter and to another man who was only a chance acquaintance. To each of them he told in detail what he expected to do the following morning. A little later, Walter Burleigh, a Dakota delegate, called to see the General only to find that gentleman dressing to attend a masked ball. The boastful old man insisted on talking to his rather reluctant guest, who had insisted on leaving, and when the caller inquired when he planned to assume his new duties, he advised that he would do so at ten o'clock the next morning and he invited Burleigh to attend this performance and see what would happen.

"But suppose Stanton objects to it and resists?" Burleigh inquired.

"Well," his garrulous friend replied, "I expect to meet force by force."

When questioned as to what he would do if Stanton barred the doors, he said, "I will break them down."

He told a reporter that same evening that if Stanton refused his demand for the possession of the office he would apply to the General-in-Chief of the Army for a force sufficient to take possession of the War Department and that he did not see how Grant could possibly refuse his demand. He happened to see this same reporter later that night at the Willard and thinking that he had not fully impressed him again made these bold threats. At the masked ball that night he bragged that he was going to take possession of the War Department the next morning and would at that time open the Department's mail.

Naturally these boasts were tasty gossip and were at once relayed to Stanton. While the General was sweating on the dance floor from over-exercising, Stanton was sweating with anxiety. Stanton that night prepared an affidavit, stating that Thomas planned to forcibly remove him and that this act was a violation of the Tenure of Office Act. Stanton further stated that Thomas was "guilty of high misdemeanor." For this cause he sought the arrest of Thomas by warrant and the paper was addressed to David K. Cartter, Chief Justice of the Supreme Court, a Radical and not unwilling tool of Mr. Stanton. The judge was found that night and he affixed his seal.

Early the next morning General Thomas was waited upon by the law officers and they informed him that he was under arrest. The old General had not had his breakfast, and he inquired of Marshal Gooding if he would be permitted to see the President, as he wanted to tell him of his arrest. The Marshal agreed but stipulated that he must not lose sight of his prisoner even for a moment. The little group went along to see Mr. Johnson, who quietly replied, "Very well, that is the place I wanted it—the courts." Thomas was advised by the President to call upon the Attorney-General and to tell him just what had happened. For some reason the Attorney-General did not grasp the importance of Thomas' arrest and the fact that it afforded a habeas corpus application to test the constitutionality of the Tenure of Office Act, but he did not. Instead he told him to go ahead to court. This Thomas did, and when he proceeded to Justice Cartter's Court, he was required to give $5,000 bail and was then discharged.

General Thomas was old and he had no one to advise him and from his former boastful state, he suddenly seemed to become befuddled and inquired of the Judge to know what it all meant. The Judge told him to present himself at 10:30 on the next Wednesday morning at his court. Then Thomas wanted to know if this arrest suspended him from the functions of his office. Quite hastily the Judge replied, "No, it has nothing to do with them."

Poor General Thomas still was without his breakfast, but he went back to the White House to advise the President of his bail. Again the President quietly replied, "Very well, we want it in the courts."

The original letters to Stanton and Thomas were dated February 21 and by midnight, **Moore, the President's** secretary, was awakened with a message from the President that General Thomas was at the masked ball in a drunken condition and the request was made that Moore go and attempt to straighten the old man out. He replied that he would do so the very first thing the next morning, but alas the next morning was too late.

After the General's second call on the President, he went at once to Stanton's office and found him almost surrounded by some six or eight Radical politicians. Thomas hesitated, saying that he did not wish to disturb the group, to which Stanton replied, "There is nothing private. What do you want, sir?"

Then the Secretary of War *ad interim* said that he demanded the surrender of the office. Stanton refused and ordered him back to his own office as Adjutant-General. Back and forward they made demands on each other to surrender the office, with Stanton alternately ordering the old General out of his office and back to his own office. Finally Stanton told the General "You can stand there as you please. I order you out of this office and to your own. I am Secretary of War and your Superior."

After this fourth exchange of official banter, the General

left the room and went across the hall to the office of another officer. Stanton followed him and handed Thomas the written order prepared the day before citing that Thomas' conduct and orders were illegal. Stanton was accompanied by some Congressional witnesses, who had been in his office when Thomas had arrived. A further dialogue continued in which Thomas was ordered to go but he refused. His fine boasts of using force had disappeared into thin air.

It was at this point that the affair betook on the nature of a complete farce. Thomas turned to Stanton and said, "The next time that you have me arrested, please do not do it before I get something to eat," and continued to decry the fact that he had had nothing to eat all that day. He did not add that he had been drunk the night before.

Stanton arose and came over to the General and put his arm around his neck, running his fingers through the General's thinning hair and sent a messenger out for a bottle of whiskey. In the meantime, he turned to General Schriver and called out, "Schriver, you have got a bottle here. Bring it out. We need it now."

General Schriver got his bottle but it had only a very little whiskey in it. Stanton took two glasses and made quite a production of measuring the whiskey out exactly evenly and he and Thomas drank together. Soon the messenger arrived, and the two were able to quench more adequately their thirst as soon as the cork was pulled.

After this was over the Adjutant-General went a third time to the White House and reported to the President that Mr. Stanton had refused to surrender the office of Secretary of War. About this time Welles, Secretary of the Navy and Attorney-General Stanbery called to tell Mr. Johnson of these same developments. The President was very disturbed. He asked the latter callers what they thought of appointing Thomas Ewing, Sr. as Secretary of War. Thomas Ewing, Sr. was the father-in-law of General Sherman, and was a Conservative statesman. They agreed and the President had his secretary, Colonel Moore, write out Ewing's nomination and Moore took the signed nomination to the Capitol to give to the Senate.

During this same interview Secretary Welles told the President of a happening that his son, Edgar Welles, had reported to him. At a party the night before given by a Mrs. Ray and attended by Edgar Welles, an orderly had appeared to require all officers of the Fifth Cavalry to appear at headquarters. Then a second orderly in full uniform had appeared to bring word that all officers under the command of General Emory, who was the Washington post commander, should report to their headquarters. The Secretary of the Navy inquired now if the President had given these orders. He had not. While the President had resorted to no extreme measures, evidently Stanton, Grant or both had issued orders which were proclaimed publicly at a social gathering and were assuming full command of the troops. There was no other assumption except that they were assuming control as a conspiracy.

The President had Colonel Moore send a message to General Emory, requesting him to call on the President. The General arrived and Mr. Johnson explained the information that he had received that morning. He inquired of him who had given the orders and what had they meant by making various changes and not reporting them to him. Emory admitted that the orders had come from the General of the Army and that a general order of the War Department had been published that all orders relating to military operations issued by the President or the Secretary of War should be issued through the General of the Army, Ulysses S. Grant.

General Emory was half insolent and half respectful. Mr. Johnson inquired of him, "Am I to understand that the President of the United States cannot give an order but through General Grant?"

To this General Emory answered that this was the opinion of some of the leading lawyers of the country. When queried as to who these might be, he named Reverdy Johnson of Maryland and Robert J. Walker.

At the break of dawn the next morning, which was Saturday, it seemed that everyone in Washington rushed to the Capitol. Washington's Birthday was to be the day to be most lamented as a blot on American history. Thad Stevens sat grinning, while Ben Wade, ascending the Speaker's platform surveyed the situation with evident satisfaction. About two o'clock Thad Stevens hobbling at the head of the Committee on Reconstruction requested that no approval or disapproval be expressed now on the report about to be made. According to the New York *World,* he arose "haggard and trembling" and offered the Committee's report: "Resolved, that Andrew Johnson, President of the United States, be impeached of high crimes and misdemeanors." It has been truthfully said that no more unjustly maligned man ever lived and it is needless to omit the name of Jesus Christ, for they were both blameless of the charges of which they were accused.

Thad Stevens declared himself to be ready for the vote without debate, but if the other side wished to speak, he insisted on the right to final rebuttal. The other side did wish to speak though they knew full well that nothing that they might say would be of avail, for the impeachment would be ordered by a strictly party vote. They debated so long that the Radicals set back the clock and ordered that Monday should appear on the House Journal as Saturday, February 22, in order that it might be recorded that the day of impeachment of the President was set on Washington's Birthday.

And what was Andrew Johnson doing during this melee? He coolly surveyed the arrangements being made and was doubtless the calmest person on Capitol Hill. On the evening of Saturday, February 22, 1868, he had planned to tender the Democratic National Executive Committee a formal dinner party. Not only did the affair come off as scheduled, but it lasted until 10 o'clock and the President and guests were described as "blandly indifferent" to all of the turmoil and dissension going on more or less like a cat and dog fight. On Sunday he was equally as calm, for though he was sometimes indecisive, he was naturally resolute, and was buoyed up by a calm belief in what was right and in an inherent belief in fate.

On Monday morning another performance was put on and the populace rushed to the House galleries. The entire Capitol police force was required to keep order about and in the Capitol Building. The Radicals combed the heavens with their rhetoric and it was not until 4:30 that Stevens walked feebly to a chair on the platform behind the Speaker's desk. He had the strength for a gleam of triumph in his eyes and to curl his lips in a sardonic smile. Every soul present was as still as the grave. The clerk proceeded with the roll call and when the result was announced, the vote was 126 for an impeachment trial and 47 against such a trial. There was no wild demonstration as expected, for it had been a strict party vote. The Republicans had been instructed on what to do and they had done it. This was in the House of Representatives only.

On the next day, which was the 25th of February, the ghastly Thad Stevens entered the doors of the Senate and the doorkeeper announced in a loud voice, "A message from the House of Representatives." Old Thad straightened his bent frame, threw his hat on the floor, handed his cane to the doorman and drew a piece of paper from his pocket. He then informed the Senate that, "The People of the United States" had impeached Andrew Johnson for high crimes and misdemeanors.

"The Senate will take order in the premises," Ben Wade announced. John Wilkes Booth in the height of his acting success could not have done better. The Senate appointed a committee of seven to draft rules for the trial and to Andrew Johnson came word of the fact that his impeachment trial had been voted.

XXI : THE IMPEACHMENT TRIAL

GIDEON WELLES, SECRETARY OF THE NAVY, had declared that the Radicals were ready to impeach the President, ". . . had he been accused of stepping on a dog's tail." The blood-curdling crime of which he was accused was that he had dared to remove a disloyal member of his own Cabinet.

Andrew Johnson had probably been made the man that he was, loyal and just in the face of all criticism, through the love and help of a woman who had loved him since she was seventeen and he eighteen. Had Thad Stevens known the romantic love of a good woman, doubtless history would have been changed.

But here again Ben Wade's wife was kept busy informing her sewing circle back in Ohio that there seemed no doubt in her mind that Andrew Johnson's conviction was inevitable. She was already preening herself for the White House.

There had been volunteers in 1861 but a call had been issued. Now no call was issued but the mails were deluged with offers from every corner of the United States with offers from soldiers volunteering to serve. John Burleigh wrote from New York saying, "Believing that you are the Commander-in-Chief of the army and navy; I beg leave to offer my services toward raising a regiment of infantry to be ready for the field in forty-eight hours after authority to organize same. . . ."

From Omaha, came an offer from James Hannan to organize a personal body guard and from Charleston, Massachusetts, came an offer to raise ten regiments. Even from Pennsylvania, state of the old commoner, Thad Stevens, came an offer of 2,000 men who had never been whipped. Indiana offered 5,000 and Kentucky's offer was for 100,000. Thirty thousand Virginians were clamoring for an opportunity to fight to preserve the Union and the Constitution.

How easy it would have been for Andrew Johnson to have had another civil war. This one would have been with no state lines, but on one side there would have been the followers of Lincoln and on the other, those of old Thad Stevens and Charles Sumner.

It is a temptation to all who read the details to regret half-heartedly that he did not put the bugle to his lips and allow arms to be taken to restore the rights of the white man and the ten Southern States to their just representation. But he reasoned that one holocaust was enough for the generation of this new and struggling nation which he loved so well. He refused the offers and chose instead to drink the bitter hemlock of defeat, if need be.

"Ben Wade will be President in a fortnight from today," so ran the gossip in Washington. Mrs. Wade sat in the gallery and smirked at all whom she thought took notice of her. Tickets were printed by Phelps and Solomon, Washington printers, and issued to some with and some without charge. They stated, "Admit the Bearer—U. S. Senate—Impeachment of the President—March 13, 1868" and were signed by Geo. T. Brown, Sergeant-at-Arms. These were numbered and taken up at the Main Entrance. Washington scarcely needed its few theaters for entertainment as this trial began on the Ides of March in the year of 1868.

On Saturday, March 7 the summons was served on the President from the Senate. He was not required by law to appear in person and he did not do so. The managers of the performance undoubtedly wanted the President to exhibit himself and the possibility was discussed by Mr. Johnson and his loyal Cabinet members. Welles insisted that for the President to appear would lend dignity to the proceedings which the conspirators wanted. The counsel chosen to represent him consisted of Attorney-General Stanbery, Benjamin R. Curtis, Jeremiah S. Black, William M. Evarts, and Thomas A. R. Nelson. All were lawyers of highest reputation and Nelson enjoyed a national reputation. Stanbery was so loyal to his chief that he told him that if he could only keep well during the length of the trial, he would be willing to be ill the rest of his life. Thomas Nelson was the least sophisticated of the group. He was a fellow towns-

of the President and had practiced his profession in his
ve town for thirty years with only a brief period in Congress, which had changed him little. In contrast to him was
William M. Evarts, a graduate of Yale, and an acknowledged
leader of the New York bar.

Horace Greeley was doing everything, through the columns
of his newspaper, to fan the blaze against the President. By
coincidence this fiery editor had married a girl in the town of
Warrenton in Johnson's native state of North Carolina in the
small Emmanuel Episcopal Church, while she was teaching in
a young ladies' boarding school. No one cared from whence
anyone came. The only struggle was to get a ticket for a seat.
At nearly midnight on the night before the trial a Senator was
aroused from his bed by a fair visitor. Going down half-dressed,
he inquired the urgency of her visit and was told that the
urgency was a ticket for the trial. He had none but she would
not agree to leave until he promised to procure one for her
somehow.

There were thirty-seven states in the Union, each entitled by
the Constitution to two senators. But the senators from the ten
Southern States were excluded and these ten states would undoubtedly have cast votes against the accusers.

At the beginning of the trial forty days were requested by
counsel for preparation of the defense. This was refused. The
President was not allowed the courtesies that would be accorded
to a pickpocket. However a short recess was allowed during
which the Senate retired for consultation. Any possible illusion
of grandeur now disappeared. The galleries thinned out, representatives lounged about and Thad Stevens sat devouring a
huge dish of raw oysters which had been brought in to him.
When the Senate returned from recess nine days were granted
for preparation instead of the forty days requested. People
ambled out as from a county court room, which often has been
known to have greater dignity.

During the darkest days of the impeachment trial one of the
President's counsel, Jeremiah Black came to see Mr. Johnson
and told him how black the outlook was. He told him that it

looked as though a conviction would follow but there was one avenue of escape from his persecutors. When Mr. Johnson inquired as to what this avenue was, Mr. Black explained that General B. F. Butler, one of the chief Radical managers of the trial, had been gathering guano from a small island known as Alta Vela. Santo Domingo claimed the island and was now objecting to this removal of fertilizer. Now General Butler had assured Mr. Black that if the President would order a "man-of-war" to go with Butler's private guano vessel that all would go well with Mr. Johnson's impeachment trial. Mr. Johnson replied that he did not believe that he had a right to issue such an order but that he would confer with the Attorney-General on the matter. Jeremiah Black returned the following day with an order signed by four of the managers, including Butler and Stevens, who was always after a fast dollar, holding that the claim was valid and that it should be enforced. Black insisted that the President sign the order but Johnson insisted that he had no constitutional right to do so and showed Black that while Black was Attorney-General in Buchanan's Cabinet he had held unconstitutional such a claim, and the President then peremptorily refused to sign the order.

Black then indignantly told Johnson: "I have pointed the way to your acquittal and advised you to pursue it. You decline to do so. You will be convicted and removed from office. I prefer not to have you convicted on my hands, therefore I resign as one of your counsel, from the impeachment case."

Mr. Johnson arose and looked at Mr. Black. "I regard your demand as dishonorable and insulting. Resign and quit. . . . It is my pleasure to accept your resignation." So Jeremiah S. Black got out as counsel for the President.

There were even more snide attempts to ridicule the President during the trial by a type of side play. A certain man named Wood from Tuscaloosa, Alabama, had on occasion presented himself to Mr. Johnson to seek employment in the government service. The President, according to Wood, had asked him if he knew of any differences between the Chief Executive and Congress. On cross examination the Attorney-General brought out that Wood had told this story to a certain Koppel, a merchant of Washington.

"Who is Mr. Koppel?" inquired Butler.

Wood answered, "Mr. Koppel is an acquaintance of mine on the Avenue—a merchant."

"What kind of merchandise, please?" insisted Butler.

Wood answered, "He is a manufacturer of garments—a tailor."

This had been planned and produced the laughter which Butler had hoped to produce.

Benjamin R. Curtis of Massachusetts opened for the defense. He had served six years on the Supreme Court bench from which he had resigned eleven years before. He had written one of the great dissents in the Dred Scott decision.

"Suppose a law should provide," Curtis asked, "that the President of the United States should not make a treaty with England. It would be a plain infraction of his constitutional power, and if an occasion arose when such a treaty was in his judgment expedient, it would be his duty to make it; and the fact that it should be declared to be a high misdemeanor, if he made it, would no more relieve him from the responsibility of acting through fear of that law than he would be relieved of that responsibility by a bribe not to act." It was a great lawyer's argument, and it was the argument of an unbiased judge. It was a plea to the intelligence rather than to the emotions.

Poor old General Lorenzo Thomas was like clay in Butler's hands. He lampooned and made fun of the old man but somehow Thomas made it plain that at no time had the President authorized him to make use of force or threats. The old man was meek and, to be fair to him, he meant no harm by his garrulous boasts. He was simply vain and confused, as well as uncertain. At the end of his testimony he said meekly to Butler, "Thank you." It was proven that Stanton had no communications with the President from August 12, 1867 until February 21, 1868 and was running the War Department without the advice of the President.

Every conceivable slander was concocted. Even Jeremiah

Black's withdrawal from the case was turned into an insinuation against the President by Butler, the very man who had tried so insistently to benefit by the Alta Vela conspiracy. Of a certain objection that had been raised by the defense, Butler stated, "Most of the objection is composed of the statements of Mr. J. S. Black . . . who refused to have anything to do with this case anyhow." As he desired, this evoked laughter from the Court.

One of General Thomas' lawyers was Cox. While Cox was on the stand, he was relating an interview with the President at five o'clock in the afternoon. Butler interrupted him by saying, "Stop a moment, I object to the statement of the President at five o'clock in the afternoon. By five o'clock in the afternoon the President, of course, would be too drunk to make any statement." Again the High Court was convulsed with laughter.

Another witness claimed he went to the White House and on occasion found the President and his son, Colonel Robert Johnson, both drunk. On cross examination, he admitted that he was mistaken about the President, but he was positive about Colonel Robert Johnson.

There was a reference to the charge that the President kept a mistress at the White House, but it did not seem to occur to anyone, that already domiciled in the White House were Mrs. Johnson, Mrs. Patterson, and Mrs. Stover, and five grandchildren, all in a structure that boasted of only six bedrooms. Where this phantom mistress was supposed to be quartered was not brought out, nor was there any attempt to name such a person who could neither be identified nor produced.

General Thomas had long since yielded to Stanton and the latter continued in office, but there was no love lost between Grant and the reinstated Secretary of War.

Butler pronounced the President's plea that he had removed Stanton for the purpose of testing the constitutionality of the Tenure of Office Act as only a base subterfuge.

Mrs. Ben Wade sat in the gallery preening herself. She had heard with pride her husband announce, as presiding officer of the Senate, "The managers of the impeachment will advance within the bar and take the seats provided for them." Six of them advanced, arm in arm, and then behind them limped Thaddeus Stevens, supported on each side by a friend, for he could no longer walk alone. Bingham had read the charges and during the reading all of the managers remained standing, except Stevens. Old age and infirmities forced him to sit.

Thomas A. R. Nelson from Greeneville, closed for the defense. He felt that high time had arrived to answer the reference to Black's withdrawal from the President's case. He now stated all of the facts of the Alta Vela affair. "These men know little of the President of the United States, far less than your humble speaker knows, who imagine that they can force or drive or compel him, under any imaginable state of circumstances, to do what he believes to be wrong. He is a man of peculiar temperament and disposition. By careful management, he may, perhaps be gently led; . . . but no power under the heavens can compel him to go one inch beyond what he believes to be right . . ."

About this time Grant told Senator Henderson from Missouri, "I have reason to believe, from good authority, that the managers of the impeachment are confident of success."

"They have no substantial grounds for such confidence," Henderson replied.

"I may tell you in confidence," Grant continued, "that not only is it expected that Ben Wade will become President but the members of his Cabinet have been selected . . . I will tell you at least that General Butler has been designated as Secretary of State."

About a week later Grant happened to board a streetcar on which Senator Henderson was a passenger. He sat down beside him and inquired if the Senator had changed his mind about the impeachment. When told that he had not, Grant asked, "Do you think that you can defeat it?"

"I cannot give a pledge that we shall actually defeat it," was Henderson's answer.

"Well I hope you won't. I would impeach him if for nothing else than because he is such an infernal liar."

Henderson looked at the small man beside him and indignantly responded, "I very much regret to hear you say it, because on such terms it would be nearly impossible to find the right sort of man to serve as President." A sword could not have cut Grant more sharply.

Garfield had described Ben Wade as a

man of violent passions, extreme opinions and narrow views; a man who had never thought nor studied carefully on any subject except slavery; a grossly profane, coarse nature who is surrounded by the worst and the most violent elements in the Republican party . . . that already the worst class of political cormorants from Ohio and elsewhere are thronging the lobbies and filling the hotels in high hopes of plunder when Wade is sworn in.

The hope of acquittal was in the Conservatives of the Republican Party. And now the churches got in on the act. The General Conference of the Methodist Episcopal Church was in session in Chicago. Bishop Simpson, a shrewd, sectarian politician, conceived the idea of bringing church influence to bear on Senator Willey of West Virginia, who was a Methodist. Simpson now set to work to bring this about and on May 13, a motion was made at the General Conference for an hour of prayer in aid of the impeachment.

There was at least one old delegate whose conscience was not dead. He proposed that the proposal be laid on the table for he explained, "My understanding is that the impeachment is a judicial proceeding and that Senators are acting under oath. Are we to pray to Almighty God that they may violate their oaths?"

The next day Simpson had thought of a variation in offering a new resolution. This resolution explained that painful rumors were circulated that certain corrupt influences had been brought to bear upon the Senators to prevent them from performing their duty. Therefore it was resolved that on the following day that an hour of prayer should be set aside to beseech God to "save our Senators from error." They thought that this would be clear to God Almighty and it is to be hoped that their hypocrisy was. (Andrew Johnson was also a Methodist.) The

Negro Methodists were more forthright. They were in conference in Washington at the same time. For fear that there might be some divine mistake—or some heavenly crossing of the wires, they prayed directly for the President's conviction and they did not bypass their petition via God, but prayed directly to the United States Senate. At least they were sincere.

Wendell Phillips spoke before the fifth annual meeting of the Anti-Slavery Society at Steinway Hall in New York City. The "great treason" of the President according to Phillips was that he had attempted to save in the South, "The white man's government . . . and the aristocratic indolence . . . this idea of a gentleman."

There had been a question of the right of Ben Wade to vote, but his fellow Senator from Ohio insisted since otherwise his state would be deprived of a vote. Wade had been ostentatiously silent on all previous roll calls. Willey of West Virginia, possibly influenced by Bishop Simpson's resolution voted for conviction. Thirty-six votes were needed for conviction. Huge bets were placed by gamblers both for and against acquittal. The paradise for gamblers was doing all right.

In an upper bedroom of the White House Eliza McArdle Johnson was waiting for the verdict. Her husband had stood up well under the strain, but there is no record that this frail woman was able to do as well as her husband. We do know that she sewed industriously throughout the waiting weeks. She was an ill woman and the mother of five children, one of whom had met a tragic death long after reaching manhood.

There were seven doubtful Senators. Ross of Kansas, Henderson of Missouri, Saulsbury of Delaware and the ill Senator Grimes of Iowa and these four all knew that a vote for the President would spell political oblivion for them. All seven of the doubtful Senators voted for acquittal and the impeachment charges were refuted by one vote.

Colonel William Crook, who was the President's bodyguard, vaulted down the steps of the Capitol Building and ran the entire length of the Avenue to reach the White House. He slammed his way into the library in which the President sat, surrounded by friends. Mr. Johnson accepted the congratulations of his friends, but the tears streamed down his face. Across the hall waited Eliza Johnson, and with a hasty knock, Crook was admitted to her bedroom, as she sat in her rocking chair. "He's acquitted," he cried out, "the President is acquitted."

Eliza managed to rise and grasp Crook's hand with her emaciated fingers, "Crook," she allowed, "I knew it, I knew he would be acquitted." She resumed her seat and began to rock gently again.

XXII : MR. JOHNSON DURING THE TRIAL

THE ORIGINAL DATE of the trial was set for March 13, 1868 but after discussions a delay of nine days was allowed to the defense for prepaartion of the President's case. The case had dragged on until Saturday, May 16.

The day before this Saturday, Mr. Johnson had presided at the dedication of Lincoln's Monument, but neither House of Congress had paid the least attention, nor had they adjourned to pay honor to the dead President.

Andrew Johnson endured his ordeal in complete silence. If bitterness and anger occupied his thoughts, he never mentioned it. His family and friends saw him come and go about his official duties.

The White House was alive with children who at least did not know that anything was amiss. Andrew Johnson, Jr., was just a youth. With Mrs. Daniel Stover, the President's second daughter, were her three children; her daughters, Sarah and Lillie, and one son, Andrew Johnson Stover. With Mrs. Patterson, the official mistress of the White House, were her two children, Mary Belle and Andrew Johnson Patterson. The President loved all children and especially his own grandchildren. He always had time to talk to them, and listen to them. His grandson, Andrew Johnson Patterson recalled that his grandfather never failed to heed their questions.

During the more than six weeks of this farcical trial, the President found some contentment with drives to Pierce's Mill on Rock Creek with the little Stovers and Pattersons. There was a pleasant meadow and the President would sit while the children gathered wild flowers or waded in the brook or hunted for water bugs. Sometimes they would engage in skipping on flat stones in the water and in this sport the President would join. In this endeavor it is quite positive that he could have out-distanced Thad Stevens.

Sometimes he and his faithful bodyguard, Colonel William Crook, would drive out into the country alone. Glenwood Cemetery was one of his favorite spots and he would stop and read the inscriptions on the headstones.

He had first insisted that he should go to the Senate Chamber but his counsel tactfully dissuaded him from this unwise course. When Butler opened for the prosecution, he again was obsessed with the idea but once more, after a conference with the men in whom he had great confidence, he was persuaded to follow their advice. Such men as Curtis, Evarts and the President's old friend and fellow townsman, Thomas Nelson from Greeneville knew Johnson's detractors well. They were thus forced to hold the trial of Caesar without the presence of Caesar.

A correspondent for the New York *World,* when questioned about an interview he had with Mr. Johnson replied, "Mr. Johnson never looked better than he does today, and his fine flow of humor indicates anything but a troubled mind."

Johnson cracked no real jokes nor told any stories, either at this time or as a usual thing during his long political life. His fame would have flourished better, probably, if he had. He did not have nor try to have Lincoln's humor. While the impeachment trial was in progress the President one day held a reception at the White House. For reasons of curiosity fifteen of the Radicals accepted his invitation. After paying their respects to the man they sought to destroy, they gathered in the East Room to compare notes. They had longed to see him wince but they were not gratified. Never once did he unbend from his grim rigidity but perhaps his eye lacked the luster of a light heart.

One of the curious of the fifteen Radicals who called that day at the White House, said to another, "What are we here for?"

"Why I want to see how Andy takes it," was the answer.

Often at night during the trial his daughter, Martha Patterson, came to the library with her chafing dish and together they enjoyed some snack or hot dish, which he especially liked.

At last the trial was over. Ben Wade's Cabinet remained on paper. Stanton immediately surrendered. General Schofield's nomination as Secretary of War was confirmed by the Senate and Stanton relinquished his place for causes stated in his note to the President. The Senate refused to confirm the reappointment of Stanbery as Attorney-General, on account of his defense of the President, as well as the name of another member of his counsel, Benjamin R. Curtis, but paradoxically accepted his third nomination for this office, who was another member of his counsel, William M. Evarts.

One personal household happening well illustrates Mr. Johnson's attitude during the trial. Slade, the mulatto steward, fell ill. The President, accompanied by his bodyguard Colonel Crook, visited Slade in his home. The aging colored man had asthma and he was struggling for breath as they entered. Mr. Johnson went up to the bed and took the sick man's hand in his. "How are you today, Slade?" he asked kindly.

Slade's death followed soon. It is easy to understand how difficult it was to spare the time but Mr. Johnson went to the funeral. The family of the dead man were deeply appreciative because the President thus honored him and Slade's daughter thanked him touchingly.

It was a well known fact that women and children could get Mr. Johnson to do almost anything at all within reason. This had been true all of his life.

XXIII : THE CARPETBAGGER REGIME

By DEFINITION A CARPETBAGGER was a Northern resident who came South after Lee's surrender, and who was able to bring all of his earthly possessions with him within the confines of a carpetbag. A carpetbag was a type of luggage of the era, with about the dimensions of the modern suitcase, but was constructed of carpet on a frame. It was a type of crude valise.

One of this dubious type of traveller, by the name of Hunnicutt, came down to Virginia. There he started a newspaper designed to bring about political control by the combined efforts of the Negro vote and those of tenant farmers, who had not joined in the fight of secession, together with the votes of fellow carpetbaggers.

Hunnicutt did a good job from his point of view but there were others who did not agree. The women of the South, no less than the male members of their families, were wont to express their opinions to friends and members of their own family circle.

In southside Virginia, a certain spinster of unquestioned refinement was Miss Frances Yarborough. A nephew of hers had fought for the Confederacy and was in the new State Legislature when it reconvened in Richmond on the advice of President Lincoln. This nephew, George Walton Hardy, had been a legislator before the War and for this reason was one of those who reconvened. He had lost his wife from the same dread disease from which Eliza Johnson suffered and his Aunt Fanny was caring for his brood of motherless children. This good lady when questioned as to what she thought of the Hunnicutt papers, vehemently replied, "It is not fit to wipe my —— on," and she pronounced the word with a broad *a*.

The Southern scalawag was a somewhat meaner man than a carpetbagger. They were slave owners and secessionists, who had turned traitor to the South before the War was over. The name originated from the story of a fellow being kicked by a sheep until he died, according to General Clanton. The man said that he did not so much mind being kicked by a sheep but he hated to be kicked to death "by the meanest wether in the whole flock—the scaly sheep." The scalawag was truly a scaly sheep.

The Union Leagues had been organized in the North for a worthy cause, to stimulate and uphold the Union cause in Ohio in 1862. Later the Union League Clubs were organized in New York and Philadelphia, but when the War ended these clubs ceased to be important in the North. The carpetbaggers used the name to organize Negroes in the South, while the reputable members in the North had no sympathy with such use of the name of their organization.

These Northern reprobates understood enough of the Negro nature to appreciate his love of ceremony and his susceptibility to superstition, which probably was an inherited tendency from the voodooism of his African forbears. These adventurers now began to organize the ex-slaves into what they called, "Union Leagues." At churches and such halls as were available, the ignorant blacks were indoctrinated by mystic rites, fires, speeches and military drills, which their leaders explained as training. Awe inspiring ceremonies were employed.

When each entered the door, a sentinel would cry out, "Who comes under our signal?" the counter sign was then asked, which was given in the four L's—the right hand pointing upward with the word Liberty, then sinking to the shoulder level with Lincoln and dropping to the side with Lord and finally folding to the breast with the word Loyal. Then they would march around arm in arm and singing *John Brown's Body* and up to an altar where stood their President, garbed in full and flashy regalia.

> John Brown's body lies a-mouldering in the grave
> John Brown's body lies a-mouldering in the grave
> John Brown's body lies a-mouldering in the grave
> As we go marching on.
>
> Glory, glory halleluia
> Glory, glory halleluia

Glory, glory halleluia
As we go marching on.

The tempo of this old martial tune was pepped up to such an extent that it was more rollicking than religious.

The altar was lavishly draped with the Union flag, where also rested an open Bible, and a copy of the Declaration of Independence. Although the Negro could not read he was told that such was the document, a sword, a ballot box, a sickle, an anvil, and any other device that could be acquired for the occasion. The Negro being by nature religious and unused to great attentions by the white man, naturally was pleased and happy in such associations.

The meetings were always in darkness, to which were added groans and the clanking of chains to increase fear and for a certain symbolism. At the last the *Star Spangled Banner* was sung and a catechism was repeated which included opposition to the Democratic Party and fealty to the Republicans, to which was added the statement that all Southern whites were traitors. Quite often the Negroes were told that in order to secure peace and "the forty acres and a mule," so much desired by them, that it would be an excellent step in the right direction to kill some of the leading whites in their community as a lesson to the others.

Always these meetings were protected by guards with shot guns to keep away intruders and the Negroes were armed also when attending these Union League meetings. It was suggested and they were encouraged to amuse themselves in military parades in the daytime and most especially to amuse themselves by pushing Southern whites off the sidewalks or crowding them off the roads.

Doubtless the Negro was not too much to blame. The white man might not have done better in like circumstances. But racial hatred was sown and the white men resolved that the Anglo-Saxon race should not be defiled. Of the Northern attitude, as reflected in the pulpit and press of Horace Greeley and others, one Southern woman wrote: "Negroes drew their own conclusions. Violation of a white woman was no harm; indeed as a leveler of social distinction it might almost be construed into an act of grace. The way to become a hero in the eyes of the white North and to win the cross of martyrdom for oneself and new outbursts of sympathy for one's race was to assault a white woman in the South."

During this era there arose a social and economic class spoken of in Virginia as "flue-cured aristocracy." This term, as explained by Mrs. Alfred Kimball Downes of Richmond, referred to the former overseer class who, knowing how to raise tobacco, after the War bought up land for the cost of unpaid taxes and made substantial fortunes.

One of these overseers truthfully stated that formerly he had made $150 annually, of which amount he had saved $100. They formed the basis of a substantial class of white citizens later.

XXIV : THE BLACK PARLIAMENT

AT LONG LAST the Southern States were all back in the union and their representatives were admitted to their seats in both houses of Congress. But it was, in many cases, a cruel farce.

The Reconstruction policy was in full force. Negro suffrage had come into vogue in full and complete force. Negro representation was in its heyday. The epitome of this was reached when the Honorable Hiram R. Revels took his seat as Senator from Mississippi. He was a Negro and occupied the seat of Jefferson Davis. Senator Wilson of Massachusetts conducted him to his seat. All Radical Senators scrambled to shake his hand and offer him personal congratulations. Sumner could hardly contain himself for his overflowing joy. Soon other Negro legislators came in the persons of Bruce to the Senate, and Rapier, Rainey and Lynch to the House of Representatives.

Negroes paraded the streets of Charleston, South Carolina, singing in loud voices, "De bottom rail is on de top, and we is gwine to keep it dar." Perhaps this truism was not a bad slogan for it indeed seemed that they were right. Soon this slogan and parading spread to other localities. There were others of the Negro race who realized this truckling to the blacks for political purposes was a false and temporary condition. Notable of these was Booker T. Washington, who then was only a youth but who later recalled that he had a feeling that mistakes were being made and that things could not remain in this condition for long.

In Mississippi, Louisiana and the Carolinas black militia were organized and the Governor of Louisiana held at his call a black standing army, the Metropolitan Guard. These states had provisional Governors.

Finally the inevitable result happened. Calvin Crozier of Mississippi, a Confederate veteran and a former prisoner of war, upon his release from a Federal jail was returning home. At Orangeburg, South Carolina he was asked by another gentleman to be allowed to place two young ladies in his charge. During the journey, Negro soldiers derailed the train and Crozier got out to investigate. When he again boarded the train he encountered two half-drunken, cursing Negro privates in his coach. One was attempting familiarities with one of the young ladies in Crozier's charge. He ejected the Negro and the other Negro joined in the scuffle. One of the Negroes ran out screaming, "I am cut by a damned rebel."

Suddenly the scene was filled with Negro soldiers, vowing and demanding revenge. That night Crozier was marched to his death. There was no trial. In the early morning he was forced to kneel at the brink of his grave and a firing party gaped as his lifeless body slumped over into the grave. The Negroes filled in the grave with earth and jumped on it, dancing and shouting with savage mirth. Thus a Confederate soldier died after being released from a Federal prison.

Occasionally the Ku Klux Klan rode and avenged a few of these wrongs, but in general they went unpunished and unabated.

Upon South Carolina fell the worst of these punishments

and indignities. Perhaps it might be reasoned this was because she was the first to secede. The dregs of society, white and black, were in absolute control. James S. Pike, who was a Republican from Maine, visited this state in the 'seventies and wrote a book aptly entitled *The Prostrate State*. His description of the "Black Parliament" is of a society turned bottomside up. After looking in at the State House one day to watch the legislature at work, he described it thus:

> A white community that had risen gradually from small beginnings till it grew into wealth, culture and refinement, and became accomplished in all arts of civilization; that successfully asserted its resistance to a foreign tyranny by deeds of conspicuous valor, which achieved liberty and independence through the fire and tempest of civil war, and illustrated itself in the councils of the nation by orators and statesmen worthy of any age and nation—such a community is then reduced to this. . . . It is the slave rioting in the halls of his master, and putting that master under his feet.

In 1872 a black Lieutenant-Governor was elected in South Carolina. Every possible plan for pilfering the public treasury was tried. Fraudulent guarantees of railroad bonds and special frauds of the printing ring increased the mounting taxes drained from an impoverished state. The State Capitol was refurnished with savage splendor. Among other articles two hundred imported china cuspidors were purchased at a cost of sixteen hundred dollars. It was indeed high-priced spittle. Six hundred dollar clocks, two hundred dollar crimson sofas and six hundred dollar mirrors were hung and arranged for comfort. A bar was added for the pleasure of the black legislators and for the more important, whiskey, cigars, brandy and champagne were added to the appropriation bills. In Columbia, South Carolina, a brothel operated by a Negro woman, was furnished at the public expense. Moses, speaker of the lower house, was voted a one thousand dollar appropriation to reimburse him for a lost bet on a horse race. Pardons were sold wholesale and when Whittemore was sent from the first district to Congress, he specialized in the sale of cadetships to West Point. During one administration, two hundred trial justices were appointed who could neither read nor write.

No white woman could go out on the street alone, even in the day time. White girls were assaulted under circumstances too horrible to describe.

Of the 124 members of the legislature, 94 were black. This was the Black Parliament. Pike described it as, "the only one on the face of the earth which is the representative of a white constituency and the professed exponent of an advanced type of modern civilization." The Speaker was black, the clerk was black, all doorkeepers were black, and the Chairman of the Ways and Means Committee was black, and the chaplain was the blackest of all. Outside of the Congo, there could not be found such types as sat at the legislators' desks.

Pike continued:

> When the legislature attempted to begin work, no one was allowed to speak for five minutes without interruption. The Negro who sat in the Speaker's chair could not suppress the general commotion. The blackest members tried to continually raise some point of order and struggled to get the floor with persistent bellowing and physical contortions, punctuated by loud guffaws. Finally the Speaker ordered a member to his seat and when the member obeyed, he immediately threw his feet on his desk so that he was hidden from the Speaker by the soles of his huge shoes.

Soon again some other member appeared again on the floor and there was a mad scramble. The Speaker threatened "to call 'the gemmun' to order." This was considered by all as a great joke and there was a loud guffaw. "The laughter continued, and while one member cracked peanuts with one hand, he used the other hand to enforce his oration from his seat." Pike said, "They laughed as hens cackle—one begins and all follow."

Horace Greeley declared, "The essential articles of the Democratic creed are love rum and hate niggers," and then continued, "I do not say that all Democrats are rascals but it is undeniably true that all rascals are Democrats." It was difficult to forget that this same Greeley had said in the month following

Sumter: "When the rebellious traitors are overwhelmed in the field . . . they must find poverty at their firesides and see privation in the anxious eyes of mothers and the rags of children." It is difficult for one to have any sympathy with him even though his own marital life was a bedlam.

With all this Andrew Johnson had struggled to bring about some type of justice to the Southern whites as he looked out on this Southern desolation. For this he had allowed himself to be persecuted by the Radicals and had uttered no word of complaint.

He had even attempted to have certain articles of furniture returned to Mrs. Robert E. Lee. These articles had been removed from her home at Arlington during the War, but he was prevented from doing so by Congress, who contended that it would be an insult to loyal Americans to return her own property to her.

XXV : SIDELIGHTS ON CHARLES SUMNER AND SOME OTHERS

AT THE AGE OF FIFTY-FIVE YEARS, Charles Sumner, Senator from Massachusetts, had fallen in love with some one other than himself and had married. The lady was beautiful and twenty-eight. One congratulation that he received was well worded but proved not prophetic. It congratulated him, "on the impending change which is to make the rest of your life a romance of untold happiness." After the honeymoon the couple came to Washington and lived at 322 I Street. They rented a pew at Epiphany Church and for a while all seemed well. A span of horses was purchased that had been the property of Lord Lyons. Sumner had married the beautiful Miss Hastings on October 17, 1866.

John Hay once described a dinner which he attended at the house of the newlyweds by saying, "Sumner has blood in his eye . . . arrogant, insolent and implacable." Later he wrote in his diary that Sumner had, "the fierce joy of a prophet over the destruction of the enemies of his Lord." This man Sumner was an egomaniac, needing treatment. Ten years before Stephen Douglas had inquired, "Is it his object to provoke some of us to kick him as we would a dog on the street?"

This was approximately what Preston Brooks did on the occasion after Sumner had maligned the serene Senator Butler of South Carolina, the uncle of Brooks, as having chosen the harlot Slavery as his mistress. Brooks struck Sumner on the head with his cane and rained fast and furious blows on the latter's pate until the cane was broken.

It is to be recalled that General Grant in an unusual burst of humor had said that Charles Sumner did not believe in the Bible, perhaps because he had not written it.

Near the end of 1867 it may have been that Mrs. Sumner had much the same feeling about Mr. Sumner. In late November when the Senators and Representatives returned to Washington, Charles Sumner returned with them, but Mrs. Sumner did not. She had spent a few weeks in the Hancock Street residence of Mr. Sumner in Boston, and then had taken herself to Lenox, never to return. It may have well been that she could no longer endure his enthusiastic self-esteem and his constant bland smile. One can be fairly sure that she did not enjoy his stories of his many social conquests in England and his utter lack of any emotional quality would be too much for any woman to endure for a lifetime. One thing is quite positive, she had had enough, for she never returned to gaze into his humorless face. Even Thad Stevens had said of him, "The god of his idolatry is Charles Sumner." At the beginning of the impeachment trial Sumner was attired in lavender silk trousers and a brown alpaca coat, and it cannot be successfully denied that he was a handsome man.

Stephen A. Douglas charged that Sumner had a certain speech written, committed to memory and had practiced it every night before a mirror, aided by a Negro boy holding a candle to watch the gestures. This so thoroughly annoyed his fellow boarders in the adjoining rooms that they were forced to quit the house.

He was thoroughly familiar with the classics, and never passed up an opportunity to use quotations from Latin or Greek poets, or from Shakespeare, Milton, Voltaire and Rousseau. However to know him was to be enraged and infuriated by him and he was as unpopular with his colleagues as with those with whom he differed as to opinions. His theory was to improve the legal status of the Negro, but any physical appeal of the Negro did not exist with him. In this respect he was the opposite of Thad Stevens. It could not be said that there was a "Miss Smith" in Sumner's life.

Benjamin Butler had been a Massachusetts Democrat. He had been military governor of New Orleans, at which time he had issued an order in regard to the women of New Orleans that had earned him the sobriquet of "Beast Butler." In this city also he had been nicknamed "Silver Spoon" or just "Spoon" due to his supposed appropriation of some Southern table silver.

He resembled a cross between a pig and a peacock more than a beast, for he was short, thickset and strongly built. He was completely bald, which gave him the appearance of having a high forehead, not properly his own. His manner was abrupt, extremely pompous and he strutted sitting down. Lincoln once said of this man that he was, "as full of poison gas as a dead dog." On one occasion in 1862, a Southern sympathizer had taken down the United States flag from the Mint in New Orleans. Butler promptly had the man shot.

On another occasion while Butler and an aide were walking through the streets, several ladies of New Orleans turned their backs upon them so swiftly that they threw their skirts in a regular circle like, "the pirouette of a dancer." Butler called out so loudly as to be clearly heard by them, "Those women evidently know which end of them looks the best."

A banquet was given in the Louisiana Capitol in honor of

the Negroes and the toastmaster was a Negro. Unconsciously the toastmaster proposed the following: "Here's to General Butler who has a white face but he has a black heart."

In 1864 when in command in North Carolina, he was removed from command when he failed to secure the Fort at Wilmington, when it was within easy reach. While in New Orleans he had made a requisition on a bank for $80,000 but after the War was over he repaid the money only to avoid a suit, and he was a spoilsman of the lowest order.

After an early Democratic allegiance, he went over to the Republican party and was received by the Radicals with open arms.

It was Senator Pomeroy of Kansas, known as Subsidy Pom, who had claimed during the impeachment trial that he had seen Mr. Johnson drunk, but later repudiated it, saying that it was the President's son who was not sober, but he claimed untruthfully that the President kept a mistress in the White House.

However before the trial was over, it was proven through an effort to besmirch Ross of Kansas that Pomeroy had offered his vote and those of several of his caucus to the friends of the President for $40,000 and his brother-in-law was his agent. This evidence was substantiated by a letter of Pomeroy's dated April 16. Also included in this prospective bargain was the award of the postmastership at Leavenworth to a certain Legate.

Lies had been told, bribes had been offered, criminals had been brought in, the President's bank account had been examined, spies had been placed in the White House in order to testify against this man, Johnson, but in the last analysis there were not quite enough thieves and his detractors were a little short of sufficient liars to convict, but they only lacked enough by one vote.

They had been so feverishly busy that when former president Buchanan died in Lancaster the House refused to adjourn during the funeral and the Senate declined to appoint a committee to attend the funeral.

Yet in 1866 Robert E. Lee had written: "Everyone approves

of the policy of President Johnson, gives him his cordial support and would, I believe, confer on him the presidency for another term, if it was in his power." Doubtless this exemplified the opinion of Virginia.

Ross of Kansas, a senator who cast a deciding vote for the acquittal of Johnson, now saw nothing that could save his political future. His old neighbors refused to speak to him and he found life in Kansas intolerable. He was later made Governor of New Mexico, a territory which did not become a state until 1912.

XXVI : PRESIDENTIAL NOMINATION OF 1868

THERE IS GRAVE DOUBT that Andrew Johnson personally desired the presidential nomination of his party in 1868, but he did nourish a hope of vindication at the polls. His opponents were legion; George H. Pendleton of Ohio, who had been McClellan's running mate four years before, sphinx-like Horatio Seymour, who presided at the convention, Senator Hendricks of Indiana and General Hancock. Considered the most formidable one in the beginning was Chief Justice Chase. His daughter, the incomparable Kate Chase Sprague, was manager of her father's campaign. By early June there were demonstrations for Chase, which seemed to be under the direction of Seymour, but the latter was felt to be subtle and not always sincere. A secret meeting was held in Philadelphia ostensibly to further the campaign of Chase, but even at that time Welles was suspicious that Seymour meant to be nominated and that his moves and those of his friends were deceptive.

Before the Democratic Convention met, the charming Kate Sprague was so zealous in electioneering for her father that Chase tried to moderate her efforts by saying to her, "Don't do or say anything which may not be proclaimed from the housetops."

Johnson had plenty of friends who were equally as determined. "Gentleman George" Pendleton had come from Ohio in linen cap and linen duster to sponsor the idea of using the depreciated wartime legal notes instead of gold in payment of the national debt. His slogan: "The same currency for the bond holder as the plow holder" was called the Ohio idea and with this his followers hoped to stampede the convention.

Vanlandingham of Ohio, a notorious Copperhead, threw his support to Chief Justice Chase. A Copperhead was a Southern sympathizer in the North during the War. As such he was the opposite of a Scalawag in the South and enjoyed about the same reputation.

On July 4, 1868, Andrew Johnson had issued an amnesty proclamation which embraced a full pardon to all who had participated in the late insurrection, except those under indictment for the offense of treason against the United States. Only one man remained to whom this pardon did not extend, and he was Jefferson Davis, who was still on bail.

On the first ballot "Gentleman George" Pendleton led with 105 votes to Johnson's 65 votes, with others trailing and Chase receiving none at this time. The President was much cheered but Gideon Welles thought that most of his votes came from the South. The balloting went on for three days with finally North Carolina, Johnson's native state giving her nine votes to Horatio Seymour, who was a former Governor of New York.

To add to the farce of the Society of St. Tammany and the Tweed Ring, the Southern delegates appeared with long hair and slouch hats. Not the least of the picturesque were the Spiritualists, with their "batteries" to hurl invisible missiles against the delegates in the sweltering heat of New York City in July. They hoped to secure Andrew Johnson's nomination and Mrs. C. A. Coleman set up her vigil within five rods of Tammany Hall and did not cease her labors day or night. Another trance medium, Amy Genner, was at work and a Mrs. Stotts was quite near Tammany Hall with her supposed divine machinations. Johnson was not a Spiritualist.

Mr. Johnson's advisers insisted that he make certain in his Cabinet; to which entreaties he replied, "I am not ambitious for further service . . . of further endurance in that elevated and responsible position, unless by a call so general and unequivocal that it would serve as a plain endorsement by the people of my endeavor to defend the Constitution. . . ."

If New York and Pennsylvania had united at any time on July 6, the President's nomination would have been insured. Seymour carefully explained to Johnson's managers how the nomination could be secured for the President. They believed in Seymour but it developed later that Chase's managers had been told approximately the same thing by Seymour. Suddenly on July 9, Seymour was nominated and soon thereafter it was made unanimous. Colonel Moore, Mr. Johnson's secretary, stated in his diary that the President "felt the disappointment keenly" but the next day he was in brighter spirits, since the suspense was over. At least one occupant of the White House was relieved and doubtless glad to be assured of the certainty of leaving Washington and she was Eliza Johnson. She was weary and only wanted to be allowed to return to her native Greeneville. The chief happiness that she experienced during her sojourn as the First Lady was her attendance at one birthday party for children on the occasion of the sixtieth birthday of her husband. On this occasion she wept tears of happiness.

As to Chief Justice Chase, he received the news of Seymour's nomination by telegram while playing croquet. After asking, "Does Mrs. Sprague know?" and being told she did, he inquired, "And how does she bear it?" When assured that she was calm in her disappointment, the old man continued with his game of croquet. His hope of the presidency had disappeared but he still liked croquet. When Seymour learned of his final defeat in the November election he wept like "an unweaned baby."

That summer Thaddeus Stevens could no longer keep himself alive with brandy. He had once inquired of the boys who took him back and forth to his seat in the House of Representatives, "Who will take me in when you boys die?" He was seventy-six and he was too weak in August to return from Washington to Lancaster. Miss Smith, his colored housekeeper, came to be with him at the end and by his own request he was buried in a colored cemetery in Lancaster. Charles Sumner was a pallbearer.

During the campaign Seymour made no speeches and neither did Grant, but he was pictured by his managers as a grim fighting man. Grant's war record and Seymour's lack of one, overwhelmingly elected the General. Grant had done the right thing for Grant in the impeachment proceedings.

XXVII : THE LAST NINE MONTHS FOR THE JOHNSONS

THE IMPEACHMENT PROCEEDINGS were over on Saturday, May 16, 1868, and the administration of Andrew Johnson did not terminate until March 4, 1869. The actual voting on all of the articles of impeachment extended until May 26 but the vote remained the same. Thirty-five Senators answered "Guilty" and nineteen answered "Not Guilty" to the roll call and thirty-six were needed to convict. All the pressure on Ross of Kansas, considered the most doubtful Senator did not prevail, although there was talk of kidnapping him by the Radicals.

In the halls of Congress later, Ross was shunned as if he were a leper. Later when he left the Senate desperately poor, he managed to eke out a scanty livelihood running a country newspaper in Coffeyville, Kansas. It seemed however, that the elements were conspiring with the Radicals for a cyclone destroyed his newspaper office and he died, old and poor some forty years later in New Mexico. Such sometimes is the reward for doing according to the dictates of one's conscience.

There was work to be done during these last months of the administration, but it is also true that Mr. Johnson did not grieve or feel the least crestfallen after the trial was over. His last months in the White House were not all toil, trouble and politics. He was eager to give joy to all that he could by entertaining all ages in the White House.

On the Thursday before Labor Day he went with one of the members of his Cabinet to a German *Schützenfest* at which he was received with great courtesy and enthusiasm. He tried a shot in a contest and was made an honorary member of the association.

On Christmas Day he issued his final amnesty proclamation, which gave without condition to everyone who might yet be under penalty because of the War of Secession a full restoration of all rights, privileges and immunities by the Constitution. This proclamation included Jefferson Davis, and ended any possible further talk of prosecuting the former President of the Confederacy. It is to be remembered that until this date Mr. Davis was at liberty on bail of $100,000.

December 29, 1868 was the President's sixtieth birthday. On that day at the White House there was a great children's party in honor of his grandchildren. Engraved cards were sent out to households throughout the city announcing that, "The President of the United States" desired their presence. All the children at Marini's Dancing Academy were invited. According to Colonel Crook, "There never had been a children's party so wonderful."

Mr. Johnson attired in frock coat and striped trousers stood at the entrance to the Blue Room and greeted his small guests with open arms. His face was beaming and his eyes smiled with affection as the children were presented to him in groups. It may well have been the first children's party that he had ever attended. On each side of him stood his daughters, Mrs. Patterson and Mrs. Stover. Mrs. Johnson also was present, departing from her usual custom. She was dressed in black, with a lace cap falling to her shoulders. She sat in a large arm chair to receive the children and observers reported that she smiled through tears at the happy children. Grant's children were invited but he forbade them to attend.

The White House was described as looking like a fairy

land for the occasion. It was brilliantly illuminated and was decorated with japonicas and azaleas. The East Room was turned over to the miniature dancers and Marini's best pupils exhibited their fanciest steps. Among the dances were a "Highland Fling" and the "Sailor's Hornpipe." Belle Patterson, as well as the two little Stover girls, Sarah and Lillie, were there running, jumping and hanging on their grandfather's arm. Surely he was the most wonderful man in the world to all of his small admirers. Finally there was the Virginia Reel, after which the President led the way to the dining room for refreshments. Little Mary DuHamel remembered for all the years of her life, "gorgeous refreshments of ice cream and cakes and beautiful glace fruits." Surely "these simple people from Tennessee" were not at a loss as how to entertain either the present or the future electorate.

New Year's Day was the occasion of another great reception. The newspapers just three days before announced that General and Mrs. Grant had left Washington to spend the New Year in Philadelphia. It was a convenient way to avoid calling on the President on New Year's Day, as was the custom. It is indeed doubtful if the former tailor in the White House felt snubbed at this discourteous behavior on the part of the former leather goods store clerk. As if to deride this rudeness Washington came to the President's New Year Reception in such numbers as never before. By noon there was such a jam of diplomats, ministers, and politicians that it was virtually impossible to get in or out of the doors. From eleven in the morning until late in the evening there was a steady stream of people, calling to pay their respects. All this was in spite of a disagreeable rain. There was one person who was probably not expected, Benjamin Butler. The President did not fail to show him formal courtesy and grasped his hand cordially.

In spite of all this the Senate on at least eight occasions thrust aside the President's nominations for ministerial appointments. Grant and Seymour had been nominated for the presidency by the Republican and Democratic parties respectively and Grant was President-elect on New Year's Day in 1869.

The last presidential reception was held on the evening of March 3, 1869 at which time the White House was again jammed with hundreds of friends, officials and ministers calling to pay their respects to the departing President. The crowd was so large that many were forced to drive away without obtaining entrance.

On March 1, it had become known that Grant had made the statement that he not only would not ride in the same carriage with the President but that he would not even speak to him. A plan was evolved to have two carriages and even two processions were proposed.

Down Pennsylvania Avenue came the Inaugural Procession. Fully two-thirds of those assembled were Negroes, who had come down from Baltimore and from the outlying districts. Finally Grant drove up to the Capitol in a dog cart accompanied by Rawlins, his old chief of staff.

Andrew Johnson's last public act was a message to the American people. It was sped over the telegraph wires as General Grant took his oath of office. It was a simple and sincere plea for peace and justice for all. Just before General and Mrs. Grant, the former Julia Dent, drove down the Avenue, Mr. Johnson and his ex-ministers, who had been with him all morning, entered the carriage of the President at the portico of the White House and were driven away.

XXVIII : JUST AFTER THE WHITE-HOUSE DAYS

ANDREW JOHNSON WAS A PRIVATE CITIZEN for the first time in forty years. His public life had begun as an alderman in the town of Greeneville in 1829 and more exactly he became a public servant when he was elected to the lower house of the Tennessee Legislature in 1835.

When he drove away quietly from the White House at noon on March 4, 1869, he was driven to the residence of a long-time friend, John Coyle, one of the owners of the *National*

Intelligencer. He actually stayed with the Coyles for twelve days. Mrs. Patterson and her family visited for a short time with the Welles family for Andrew and Eliza Johnson did not wish to inconvenience the Coyle family with the extensive household of the President's family. The entire family was to stay in Washington two weeks longer in order to procure some needed articles to make the Johnson home in Greeneville habitable. This was necessary for their home had not been occupied as a family home by the Johnsons since its occupation by Confederate troops. Johnson had not seen his old home since 1861.

Mr. Johnson had been offered several proposals of European tours, but elected, rather, to return to his home in Greeneville with his very ailing wife, whom he did not wish to leave, and who most certainly was not physically able to accompany him on a tour. English, French and German steamship companies offered him passage on their lines for himself and family. He declined all of these with grateful thanks.

However the city of Baltimore especially desired to honor this man, and he accepted this invitation. A group of well known Marylanders came to Washington to escort him there. Accordingly business was laid aside in Baltimore on March 12 and upon the arrival of the President, Camden Station was crowded with an enthusiastic and applauding throng. A troop of cavalry and a battery of field artillery stood at attention and a large band played martial airs when he descended to the square. He entered an open carriage drawn by four splendid gray horses and a grand parade started from the station. Along the streets, were crowds of men, women and children, shouting and waving flags, in a sincere impromptu demonstration of affection for this man. The parade stopped at the Post Office Building and he stood in the rotunda of that building from one to three in the afternoon to shake hands with his friends and admirers.

That night at Barnum's Hotel a great banquet was held. Prior to this, a great levee had been held in the afternoon when a number of young ladies stepped up to shake his hand. The President showed a trait of character never before demonstrated, by kissing each of them on the cheek while the spectators seemed to enjoy the occasion of this operation as much as the President himself. When the banquet was held that evening covers were laid for 275 guests. A toast was made as follows:

Our guest—the patriot statesman, Andrew Johnson, as President of the United States, the bulwark of equal rights, the champion of the only true and permanent Union of the United States, and the defender and martyr of the Constitution. History will vindicate his fame, and record the impeachment of his impeachers. . . . Baltimore bids him welcome to a place in the hearts of a great people. . . . We look with great assurance to his future efforts and influence for the liberation of the captive states of the Union and the rescue of their now true and faithful citizens from political slavery. . . .

To this Mr. Johnson made a grateful rejoinder and concluded: "My deliverance has been the greatest case of emancipation since the rebellion commenced." On the following day he returned to Washington where he and his family remained until March 18.

When they began their homeward journey the President's family consisted of Mr. and Mrs. Johnson, Robert and Andrew, Jr., Senator and Mrs. Patterson and their two children, Mary Belle and Andrew Johnson Patterson. The Stovers had already returned to Tennessee.

At Lynchburg, Virginia, he and his party were entertained at a sumptuous reception in his honor. There was also an impromptu reception at Bristol and the train had to stop at practically every station after entering Tennessee, so that his friends might see and hear their long time friend and hero. At Limestone, someone in the crowd shouted that the people of Tennessee wanted him as Governor of his state again. Johnson turned to a newspaper reporter and remarked: "Yes, there is a good deal of life in me yet." He was just past sixty.

The town council of Greeneville, of which body Andrew Johnson had been a member as far back as 1829, met on March 17 and passed a resolution that it would go to the station in a body to welcome their most distinguished citizen. But here again the Radical Mayor insisted that such a reception would show an indorsement of Johnson's policies and he vetoed the council's resolution.

In spite of this the populace came to the station in crowds. Four pretty girls—Lulu Evans, Maria Harmon, Bert and Kitty Crawford, granddaughters of old friends of the former President, presented him with great bouquets of flowers and these young ladies led the procession that escorted the Johnson family to the home of a friend. On an open porch of this home, addresses of welcome were made, to which he responded. He said in true sincerity: "I am proud to come among old friends . . ." but at the last he added with perhaps a touch of weariness and disillusionment, "An old man, weary with the cares of state, has come to lay his bones among you."

Soon there was speculation as to what he might do in the future. Would he go into retirement or re-enter Tennessee politics? There was a rumor that he planned to organize a bank or that he might open a wholesale and retail tailoring establishment.

Andrew Johnson had been frugal all of his life and one does not often basically change such habits. By this practice and prudent investment he had amassed what was considered a considerable fortune for those days. In the spring of 1869 when he returned to the town into which he had walked leading a cow in the fall of 1826, he had an estimated fortune of $150,000.

He began to improve his property and soon bought a large brick building as an investment. His fellow townsmen would notice him as he walked the streets, always with his hands behind his back, dressed in immaculate black and with a silk beaver hat resting on his head, usually bent in meditation.

He was said always to be cordial to any visitor in his home but he seldom went to the homes of others. It is a matter of interest that Mr. Johnson was a Mason, and became a Royal Arch Mason and Knight-Templar.

XXIX : THE GROWLS OF GRANT

THE PEOPLE OF WASHINGTON had not failed to observe the gruffness and rudeness of President-Elect Grant toward Mr. Johnson between the time of his election and his inauguration in March, 1869. He had left the city once to avoid attending a reception at the White House and he had forbade his children's attendance there when hundreds of other children enjoyed the hospitality of the President. Furthermore he had publicly stated that he would not only refuse to ride in the carriage with Andrew Johnson, but that he would not even speak to him. All this had been said and done by a man who only ten years before had been a clerk in a leather and hardware store at an annual stipend of eight hundred dollars.

Perhaps he had come up the ladder too fast. Most certainly he had begun his administration with a grievous blunder. At that time, A. T. Stewart was known as the most successful merchant in the United States and perhaps was one of the richest men in America. He was considered a merchant prince. He had helped Grant greatly in the campaign. Grant had been given a $30,000 home, which had been paid for by public subscription, while Johnson four years before had refused the gift of a horse and carriage which had been made by the public. A few days before President Grant took office this publicly subscribed home was repurchased by a group of friends for $65,000 and Mr. Stewart handed a check for this sum to Grant, who had accepted it. The purse had been made up by A. T. Stewart and other rich men. Now Grant nominated this merchant prince as Secretary of the Treasury, and the nomination was promptly confirmed. Some adept lawyer discovered that a law passed in Alexander Hamilton's time forbade such an appointment because Stewart was concerned in "trade or commerce." At once Grant requested Congress to exempt Mr. Stewart but Congress refused this baseless request. Necessarily Mr. Stewart's name was then withdrawn and Mr. Boutwell, one of the impeachment managers, was named in his place.

Hamilton Fish was an old man, who had once been Governor of New York, but he had taken no part in public affairs for the past ten years. However he had entertained Grant in his New York City mansion and his picturesque home on the Hudson. He was made Secretary of State and was probably the best of Grant's appointments.

Another wealthy man was Adolphe E. Borie of Philadelphia. He had once headed a scheme to present Grant with a Philadelphia home. Even Admiral Farragut had never heard of him when Borie was appointed Secretary of the Navy. At least the Cabinet was not poverty stricken. If necessary they could indeed be depended upon to provide a loan to one who had been wont to borrow in the past.

Grant's National Committee had levied heavily on the land-grant railroads and any beneficiary of the Radical bounty. The army was outfitted in new uniforms and although the depreciated war time currency was not so plentiful as formerly, there was no economy practiced in appropriations. Grant had been in office a few weeks, when at the insistence of Benjamin Butler, the Tenure of Office Bill was repealed by the House of Representatives. In order to force this action in the Senate, President Grant announced that he would make no appointments nor suspensions as long as this law remained on the statute books. There was much turmoil and many compromises before this embarrassing law was finally removed, for senators and representatives enjoyed this curb on the appointing power.

XXX : MR. JOHNSON RE-ENTERS POLITICS IN TENNESSEE

WHEN GRANT WAS NOMINATED for the presidency for the second time in 1872, Andrew Johnson again entered politics. Grant was opposed this time by the Democratic nominee, Horace Greeley of New York. The time of liberalism had not yet come. Thomas Nast ridiculed Greeley as the associate of rebels. The eccentric apparel worn by the old editor was excellent material for a cartoonist and was used without mercy. The country had prospered and apparently didn't care if President Grant had been overly fond of gifts. He rode serenely along on the wave of the post-war boom in the North. To add to Greeley's other troubles, he was called to the bedside of his dying wife and she was buried before the election. Greeley's defeat was the most decisive ever recorded for the Democrats. He carried only six states, all of these in the South, and included Tennessee. Doubtless the States of the former Confederacy were remembering that this man Greeley was the first of the suretors to sign the bail bond of Jefferson Davis.

In April 1869 a Confederate soldier, Colonel E. C. Reeves opened a small law office in Greeneville. He had never met Andrew Johnson, but he had had the former President pointed out to him. A few days after the opening of the law office, a gentleman entered his office with the announcement, "My name is Andrew Johnson. . . . I have called to meet you and give you welcome. . . . I have traveled the road of poverty and felt its pinch . . . if at any time you shall be in need of some financial help, just call on me and it will be my pleasure to aid you. Good day." Mr. Johnson's visits to this office became more frequent and culminated in Colonel Reeves becoming Mr. Johnson's private secretary.

It was Colonel Reeves, himself an attorney, who said that although Mr. Johnson was not a licensed attorney he was withal a great constitutional lawyer.

In 1872, Tennessee had been accorded an additional member-at-large of Congress by a redistricting bill and it had been authoritatively announced by a Nashville newspaper that Mr. Johnson would be the candidate. However the night before the Democratic Convention, Johnson dispatched Colonel Reeves with instructions that he would not be a candidate. He explained to Reeves that such a candidacy would interfere with his plans to run for the United States Senate in 1875. Therefore Reeves was astounded to learn on his way home from the Convention that Johnson had announced his candidacy as an Independent. For some reason the former President had been over-persuaded to accept this nomination.

It was a fierce and furious campaign. A story is told that Johnson after making a speech, had driven to the Tennessee River to cross it and catch a train. When the ferry, on which he was making the crossing, ran aground, he jumped into the river and waded to the bank. That afternoon he reached Chattanooga in time to appear on the platform with his two competitors.

However Maynard, candidate of the Radical Republicans, was elected. This was only the second defeat of Johnson's life at the polls, the first being after his first term in the Tennessee State Legislature, when he ran for a second term.

The next year in 1873 cholera raged in eastern Tennessee. Mr. Johnson could have taken his family out of the range of this dread disease, but he felt that this was not an example to be set and he remained in his home town. As a result he came down with the disease and, for many weeks, was at the point of death. He recovered but never again enjoyed his former health.

A panic ensued in 1873 and among other banks that failed was the First National Bank of Washington, which had on deposit $73,000 of Mr. Johnson's savings. There was much discussion by the press of this loss, until finally the former President published a statement that even if the whole amount was lost, he would have enough left for his needs. In spite of this Colonel Reeves, at the time of Mr. Johnson's death said that he was the wealthiest person in Greeneville. It was generally believed that he had invested in railroad securities when the railroads were young and had prospered through their growth. Later the banks repaid Mr. Johnson's deposits in full, although some of this amount was paid to his estate after his death.

When Mr. Johnson started his campaign for the Senate in the fall of 1874, it was not generally thought that he had a chance. He covered Tennessee from Bristol to Memphis. On one occasion on his arrival in Columbia to speak, he learned that an opponent had secured the Courthouse in which to speak, and was talking against time in order to prevent his speech. He instructed two men to secure goods boxes to be placed under the Courthouse window from which he spoke. In usual fashion pistols were displayed on the table before him, which he probably enjoyed. Bate, an opponent was within one vote of being chosen by the State Senate at one point, but the next day Johnson secured three new votes and was chosen by a majority of one to return to the United States Senate.

Soon after he had been advised at his room at the Maxwell House that he had been elected, Mr. N. B. Spears, a giant-like member from Marion County, entered and seized Mr. Johnson, flung his feet high in the air, and trotted around the floor with the former President so situated, apparently entirely forgetful of the dignity of the Senator-Elect. Such were politics in Tennessee in 1874. Business men rushed into the streets and joined in triumphal shouts, in this city of Nashville, in which a reckless writer had falsely proclaimed that as Military Governor this same man had "filled the jails" with Confederates. Only twelve years had passed since this charge had been made.

There was a great deal of speculation as to how the newly elected Senator would conduct himself when he returned to Washington. His hair had become slightly thinned but there was not any trace of baldness. His expression was one of a mixture of sadness and earnestness.

Sumner was dead. Thad Stevens' soul had gone to whence it would not be hampered by a club foot. Ben Wade had given up politics to become the counsel for the Northern Pacific Railroad. Of the seven doubtful Senators who had voted to acquit Johnson, the ill Grimes, who had been brought into the Senate Chamber on that 16th day of May virtually on a stretcher, had passed on to his reward. The other six loyal Senators were now politically dead. The presiding officer of the Senate was Henry Wilson, who had voted for Johnson's conviction and also "for his disqualification from hereafter holding any office under the Constitution." But nearly seven years had passed before March 6, 1875 when Andrew Johnson was sworn in for a second time as United States Senator. Without embarrassment Johnson shook hands with Wilson, then Vice-President, and when he did so there burst forth a tumult of applause and cheers.

When he again approached his seat, he saw that his desk was piled high with flowers and a little page stepped up and presented him with a bouquet. To avoid any further demonstration he retired to the cloakroom but even there he was soon followed by fellow Senators all eager to shake his hand.

When he returned to his hotel a New York *Tribune* reporter inquired of him, "Will you not in your new position have an opportunity to pay off some old scores? You must have a mass of facts against many of the leaders of the parties today." To this Johnson replied, "Whatever I may have, I do not say. I have no enemies to punish nor friends to reward."

He had been interviewed in simple quarters consisting of two rooms at the Willard on Pennsylvania Avenue. Some visitor remarked to the former President that his present quarters were less commodious than his former Washington residence. To this sally Johnson replied with an unusual flash of humor, "Yes, but they are more comfortable." Age apparently was sharpening his wit.

XXXI : ANDREW JOHNSON'S LAST SPEECH

ANDREW JOHNSON HAD ONE REASON for desiring to return to the
United States Senate, other than for his vindication. He revealed
this reason a day or so after he had taken his oath of office
to his old friend and bodyguard while in the White House,
Colonel William Crook. It was this man who had run the length
of Pennsylvania Avenue to bring the news of the acquittal to
Mr. and Mrs. Johnson. Johnson now told Colonel Crook that
he wanted to know just at what points in his scrapbooks
all the notices about Grant were pasted, as the former President
did not remember just where they could be found. Crook located them for him and Mr. Johnson then told him that he was
going to make a speech against Grant and his corruption while
in office and that he was going to make it at this session. He
made this speech on March 22. The background of this speech
was briefly thus: Fraud and embezzlement were universal.
Under the carpetbagger regime, no government except a ver-
itable state of anarchy existed. The whites in Louisiana were
greatly outnumbered by the Negroes, and this was also true in
Alabama and Mississippi.

Casey, the brother-in-law of Grant, was Collector of the Port
of Customs of New Orleans. A certain Henry Warmoth had
come into Louisiana with the Federal Army from which it was
reliably reported that he had been dishonorably discharged. He
had now made himself Governor of the proud state of Louisiana.

It had happened thus: In the fall of 1872 Warmoth had decided that it would be well for him and his followers to go over
to the Democrats and support John Enery, a Confederate veteran, as candidate for Governor. At that time Louisiana enjoyed a mulatto Lieutenant Governor, Pinchback. Now Pinchback united with Grant's brother-in-law, Casey, in the support
of William Kellogg, a carpetbagger, who had come to Louisiana
from Vermont. After the election each side claimed victory and
Warmoth set up a Returning Board to decide the election. He

and the mulatto Pinchback were members of this board. The Returning Board was vested with the power to reject returns if in its sole judgment corrupt influences had been employed. This board decided that Kellogg was entitled to the office and obtained an order from Judge Durell directing the marshall and the commander of the United States troops to take possession of the State Capitol and hold it for Kellogg. It was reported that Judge Durell was drunk when he signed the order, but it was never revoked. In February, 1873, President Grant made a speech in which he said that if Congress did not interfere in supporting the Kellogg government that he would do so. One pitched battle followed between the citizens in which fifty-nine Negroes and two whites were killed. A frequent inquiry heard in the lobby of the St. Charles Hotel in New Orleans was, "How are Negro votes selling today?" A member of the Congressional Investigating Committee was asked, "What is the price of a Senator?" "I think six hundred dollars," was the reply.

Finally on September 14, 1874 in the midst of another campaign a bloody struggle known as the Battle of Canal Street followed a mass meeting held to denounce Kellogg, which resulted in Kellogg fleeing and the rule of the carpetbagger was put down for the time.

However even this did not stop Federal interference. On January 4, 1875, a carpetbagger was reinstated by the force of Federal arms. When the state legislature met on this date the question arose as to whether the native electorate or the carpetbagger rule was in control. General de Trobriard was summoned and he presented himself in full uniform, with a sword at his side, and accompanied by two of his staff. He then called five of his soldiers and with fixed bayonets, they advanced upon five members of the legislature and expelled them from the hall.

Not even satisfied with this, Grant put General Sheridan in charge over the head of General Sherman, the General of the Army. Probably the motive behind this action was the fact that eight years before Johnson had dismissed Sheridan.

Now on March 22, 1875 Andrew Johnson arose in the Senate Chamber to denounce this military despotism.

"The President of the United States assumes to take command of the State and assign these people a governor," he said. He declared that Grant's weak excuse that the election of Kellogg had been displaced was nothing "but a gigantic fraud." If such were the case both claimants should be disqualified. "How far off is empire? How far off is military despotism?" He hinted that Grant would ride triumphantly into a third term and such was greatly feared by others than Johnson. It was general political talk. The galleries were full with a crowd who wished to be present when he turned the tables on Grant. Now they broke into loud applause. He declared, "There is a provision in the Constitution which declares that: 'No title of nobility shall be granted by the United States, and no person holding an office . . . under them . . . shall accept any present . . . from any king, prince or foreign state.' What a fortunate thing it would have been if to this last line there had been added 'or from any citizen of the United States.'" Loud laughter followed this well-aimed thrust.

But this was a day when simple standards of honesty did not prevail. In Brooklyn a three ring circus went on in the form of a judicial hearing. Henry Ward Beecher was accused of being more than friendly in his relations with Mrs. Theodore Tilton, wife of the editor of the *Independent*. Holding a bunch of white violets at which he sniffed occasionally, he tearfully denied any wrongdoing but did admit that he had often gone to the Tilton home in the absence of Tilton and on these occasions he had kissed Mrs. Tilton "very much."

This was the day of brownstone fronts. Mahogany gave way to golden oak. Chippendale and Hepplewhite were thrown into discard and replaced by sideboards of incredible design. Many of the former had been painted over, often with garish colors, particularly green. Fireplaces were bricked up and beautiful mantels were hacked away. Garish hotels in cheap imitation of the European hostelries took the place of the pleasant inns of former days. Public taste and morals became a nightmare. American hypocrisy began to blossom in full flower.

XXXII : REQUIEM

In the usual order of events Mr. Johnson would not have been sworn into office as United States Senator until December, 1875. However President Grant had convened the Senate into an extra executive session to pass upon a treaty with King Kalakaua of the Sandwich Islands. It was a most fortunate thing for Mr. Johnson that this happened. Otherwise his election to this last office would have been an empty and useless gesture by the electorate. Now two days after Johnson's fiery speech regarding Grant, Senate adjourned, and the Tennesseean returned to Greeneville never to return to Washington. Mrs. Johnson was still living and lived until January 15, 1876.

He seemed to have new strength brought on by a consciousness of a return of personal power. He was the first ex-president to return to the Senate and he was now only sixty-six years old. Perhaps he may have thought a full vindication would place him in the White House again before the final end.

He rested in Greeneville from March until July. He seemed particularly happy there with Martha Patterson, her husband and their two children. About forty miles from Greeneville, his daughter, Mary Stover, now a widow and her three children, lived in the mountains of Carter County on the banks of the beautiful Watauga River.

The last of July is always hot in the East and the weather was not unlike that of 1826 when Johnson with his cart and leading a cow had first crossed the mountains from North Carolina in September. He decided to make the trip to Carter's Station to visit the Stovers. In talking to Captain W. E. McElwee on the train that morning he had said, "More than a hundred times I have said to myself, 'What course may I pursue so that the calm and great historian will say one hundred years from now, "He pursued the right course." ' "

When the former President reached Carter's Station his daughter's buggy had not yet arrived. He was able to procure a horse from young Selden Nelson, the son of his able counsel from Greeneville in the impeachment proceedings. He had ridden along a little way when he was met by the Stover buggy and continued thus to his daughter's farm, arriving there about an hour before noon.

He had often said that when the end came, he hoped to go ". . . all at once and nothing first." Also he had said, "When I die, I desire no better winding sheet than the Stars and Stripes and no softer pillow than the Constitution of my country." Both wishes were fulfilled.

After lunch that hot July day, he sat discussing her approaching wedding plans with his granddaughter, Lillie Stover. She walked to his room with him and as she was going out, she heard a heavy thud. Mr. Johnson had fallen to the carpet with a stroke of paralysis. He was perfectly conscious the next day and fell to discussing his old tailor shop and his early political campaigns. However another stroke followed and he lapsed into unconsciousness. He lingered on a few days but on the afternoon of July 31, the great statesman died.

Plain people from the mountains filled the Stover house with mourners. On Sunday morning the family set out for Greeneville with the body. All Greeneville was draped with black. The old tailor shop was hung with mourning and flowers. On a silver plate on the casket were inscribed these words: "Andrew Johnson, Seventeenth President of the United States." He was buried on a cone shaped hill about a half mile from his home. He had himself selected this spot and now his faithful servant, Sam, was able to identify the exact location. No Emancipation Proclamation had ever separated these two friends, master and servant, friends throughout life and finally separated only by death.

With his own hand Mr. Johnson had planted, by his selected burial site, a willow from his yard, an offshoot of a tree brought from Napoleon's St. Helena tomb. About his body was draped a new flag with thirty-seven stars, while under his head was placed his well-thumbed copy of the Constitution. His son Robert had died soon after his father's return to Greeneville.

Knoxville, Nashville and Memphis had each requested the honor of becoming the final resting place of the departed statesman, but the family denied these requests preferring the soil of his beloved county of Greene.

At the head of the coffin walked his old friend Blackstone McDannel, a former plasterer of Greeneville. The procession, more than a half mile—eight blocks—in length, included the great and the humble and many statesmen from the Nation's capital and much of America were represented.

A Masonic choir chanted the requiem and a bugler sounded taps and the former Brigadier General, Andrew Johnson, slept in peace at last. Carved on the simple shaft above him today, one may read these words: "His faith in the people never wavered."

XXXIII : EPILOGUE

ON OCTOBER 19, 1948, there was unveiled in the city of Raleigh, North Carolina, an equestrian statue honoring the three presidents from that state; Andrew Jackson, James Knox Polk and Andrew Johnson. This statue presents President Jackson on his steed and Polk and Johnson are seated. The inscription is as follows:

Andrew Jackson—1829–1837
James Knox Polk—1845–1849
Andrew Johnson—1865–1869

One can look to the north in the next block and clearly see the site of the seventeenth president's humble birth place and the old State Bank Building, now Christ Church Rectory, where his father was porter at the time that Andrew was born.

On the day of the unveiling, the then President Truman made an address and stated: "Andrew Johnson was a Southerner and a plebeian. . . . If he found that a man was a liar and a scoundrel, he called him just that. . . . There is much reason to believe that except for the dogged courage of Andrew Johnson, Jeff Davis would have died on the gallows and Robert E. Lee might have died with him." One is inclined to concur with the former statement but to disagree with the latter.

On Saturday, April 26, 1958, in Greeneville, Tennessee, a formal opening of the Andrew Johnson Home and New Visitor Center was held, under the auspices of the National Park Service. Among the speakers was the Honorable B. Carroll Reece, member of Congress from the First District of Tennessee. The ribbon cutting at the home was done by the former President's great-great-great-granddaughter, Miss Corinne Patterson Colt, of New England.

To the program for this occasion I am indebted for the following record of Mr. Johnson's political and personal history:

APPENDIX : ANDREW JOHNSON, SEVENTEENTH PRESIDENT

Born, Raleigh, North Carolina, December 29	1808
Moved to Greeneville, Tennessee and established his trade as a tailor	1826
Married Eliza McArdle, May 17	1827
Elected alderman, three terms, Greeneville, Tennessee	1829–1831
Elected Mayor, three terms	1832–1834
Elected to Lower House of State Legislature	1835–1837
	1839–1841
Elected to State Senate	1841–1843
Elected U.S. Congressman from State of Tennessee and served five consecutive terms	1843–1853
Elected Governor, State of Tennessee, two terms	1853–1857
Elected U.S. Senator from State of Tennessee	1857–1862
Appointed by President Lincoln as Military Governor of Tennessee	1862–1865

Elected Vice President, March 3	1865
Became President of United States upon Lincoln's Assassination, April 15	1865
At end of his term as President returned to Greeneville	1869
Elected United States Senator	1875
Died in Carter County, Tennessee, July 31	1875

At the time of this writing May 16, 1958 the following descendants of this great man survive:

Mrs. Margaret Patterson Bartlett—Great-Granddaughter
Mrs. Martha Landstreet Willingham—Great-Granddaughter
Mrs. Belle Willingham Colt—Great-Great-Granddaughter
Mrs. J. Taylor Ellyson Crump—Great-Great-Granddaughter
Mr. Thomas Clyde Colt III—Great-Great-Great-Grandson
Mr. Jon Landstreet Colt—Great-Great-Great-Grandson
Mr. Taylor Nicholas Crump—Great-Great-Great-Grandson
Miss Corinne Patterson Colt—Great-Great-Great-Granddaughter
Mrs. Andrew Johnson Bachman—Great-Granddaughter-in-law

Calmly now one can only say, let it not be the case that: "The evil that men do lives after them, the good is oft interred with their bones."

BIBLIOGRAPHY

Beale, Howard, *Andrew Johnson, The Critical Year*. New York: Harcourt, Brace & Co., 1930.

Bowers, Claude S., *Andrew Johnson, The Tragic Era*. Cambridge: Houghton, Mifflin Company, 1929.

Bradford, Gamaliel, *Wives*. New York: Harper & Bros., 1925.

Colman, E. M., *Seventy-five Years of White House Gossip*. New York: Harper & Bros., 1925.

Crook, Wm. M., *Through Five Administrations*. New York: Harper & Bros., 1910.

Crook, Wm. M., *Andrew Johnson, Raleigh Commission for a Memorial*. Raleigh: Graphic Press, 1949.

DeWitt, David Miller, *Andrew Johnson*. New York: Macmillan and Company, 1903.

Hale, William Harlan, *Biography of Horace Greeley*. New York: Harper & Bros., 1950.

Kane, Harnett T., *Lady of Arlington*. New York: Doubleday & Co., 1954.

Keckley, Elizabeth, *Behind the Scenes*. New York: G. W. Carleton & Co., 1868.

Milton, George Fort, *Age of Hate*. New York: Coward-McCann, 1930.

Pike, James, *The Prostrate State*. New York: Appleton & Co., 1954.

Rives, F. J., & G. A. Bailey, *Andrew Johnson, President of the United States*. Washington, D. C., 1868.

Stone, Irving, *Love Is Eternal*. New York: Doubleday & Co., 1954.

Stryker, Lloyd, *Andrew Johnson*. New York: Macmillan and Company, 1930.

——*Andrew Johnson, Military Governor of Tennessee*. Princeton: Princeton University Press, 1916.

INDEX